MW00937037

THE BEST DIET
BEGINS IN
YOUR MIND

Other Books by Dr. Forman

Do You Use Food to Cope? A Comprehensive 15-Week Program for Overcoming Emotional Overeating

Self-Fullness: The Art of Loving and Caring for Your "Self"

THE BEST DIET
BEGINS IN
YOUR MIND

*Eliminate the Eight
Emotional Obstacles to
Permanent Weight Loss*

SHEILA H. FORMAN, PH.D.

THE BEST DIET BEGINS IN YOUR MIND
ELIMINATE THE EIGHT EMOTIONAL OBSTACLES
TO PERMANENT WEIGHT LOSS

iUniverse books may be ordered through booksellers or by contacting:

iUniverse
1663 Liberty Drive
Bloomington, IN 47403
www.iuniverse.com
1-800-Authors (1-800-288-4677)

Photo by Starla Fortunato.

ISBN: 978-1-4917-5964-6 (sc)
ISBN: 978-1-4917-5963-9 (e)

Library of Congress Control Number: 2015901564

Print information available on the last page.

iUniverse rev. date: 2/26/2015

To the women and men who
are courageous enough to put
down the food and face their
emotions. You are my heroes.

DISCLAIMER

The information, ideas, and suggestions in this book are not intended as a substitute for professional advice. You should not undertake any diet/exercise regimen recommended in this book before consulting your personal physician. Before following any suggestions contained in this book, you should consult your health-care providers and mental health professionals. Neither the author nor the publisher shall be liable or responsible for any loss or damage allegedly arising as a consequence of your use or application of any information or suggestions in this book.

In addition, throughout this book you will find case studies. Each case study is a composite of several people and situations. This is done to provide you with an illustrative example of the topic being discussed without revealing the details of anyone's life in particular. Any resemblance to any person, dead or alive, is merely a coincidence.

C O N T E N T S

PREFACE

My first career was as an attorney, and I got through law school by eating peanut M&M's. Those delicious, crunchy chocolate treats helped me ace my exams, but at the time, I didn't pay much attention. It wasn't until a decade later when I went to graduate school to study psychology and didn't need to munch on sweets to get through the course work that I began to question what was different. Thus began my interest in the relationship between eating and emotions.

I came to understand that, when I was in law school, I was unhappy, unfulfilled, pursuing the wrong career for me, and generally miserable. To survive the demands of law school, I relied on my candy-shelled friends. I didn't know it then, but I was using food as a way to cope with stress and tension. And I wasn't the only one.

I remember the last day of first-year finals when a classmate sitting behind me tore open a monster-sized bag of peanut M&M's. I could hear the tear and smell the aroma. I knew what he was doing. I, for one, could not eat during an exam, but he could. Three hours later, when the professor asked us to hand in our papers, I turned to collect his and noticed that the entire bag was finished. I knew what he'd done but, at that moment, not why he'd done it. Now I do.

Graduate school taught me a lot. First, I did not need food to get through the rigorous process. Unlike during law school, I was happy to be there. I loved my course work, the material came easily to me, and I knew I was in the right place. Sure it was stressful, but this time, I could cope with the stress directly. I didn't need any food to assist me.

This insight led me to do my doctoral dissertation on the relationship between coping skills and binge eating. I turned what I learned from that research study into my book *Do You Use Food to Cope? A 15-Week Comprehensive Program for Overcoming Emotional Overeating*. That book launched a twenty-year career in treating people with eating and weight issues.

So I come to you now with decades of personal and professional experience dealing with emotional eating and how to overcome it. I have condensed my life's work into teaching you how to overcome eight specific emotional obstacles. I am confident that, if you are able to master these obstacles, any others that come your way should be no trouble at all.

BEFORE YOU BEGIN

Hello, and welcome to a journey that could change your life. What you are about to read and experience has the potential to truly make a difference. But I feel I must caution you before you begin. All change requires work.

There are no quick fixes—at least none that last. What I am going to ask you to do is apply daily, consistent effort. This is not about perfection, but it certainly is about progress. Take the time necessary to study, understand, and apply the ideas I present. Over time, you will develop an entirely new approach to food and eating.

Along the way, you may experience emotional upheavals. You will be breaking what could be lifelong habits around food and emotions. At times you may feel moody, irritable, even grief stricken. That's understandable. After all, you are uprooting the rhythm of your life and exchanging it for a new melody, and that can be unsettling.

Keep in mind that this is not about willpower. Rather, it is about mind power—the power of your mind to heal the emotional triggers that send you to the food. I can tell you that it does get easier.

Your new ways of dealing with your emotional life will become your new habits, which in turn will become your new normal—a slimmer, healthier normal. For every health-ier choice you make, you will become free to be a new, dif-ferent, and better person.

As with any journey, you cannot truly begin until you are ready. So do what you need to do to get ready to change your habits, and, when you have, turn the page.

INTRODUCTION

You don't have to be a rocket scientist to know that you have to eat less and exercise more to reach the weight that is right for your body. But it takes more than knowing that truth to achieve your weight-loss goals. It takes a willingness and ability to stick to whatever plan or program you have chosen—no matter what. To do that you need to have your mind and your emotions on the same page. Too many best-laid plans have been derailed because of out-of-control feelings and emotional pain. This book is designed to help you avoid those pitfalls as you pursue your current (and final) weight-loss attempt.

Learning to manage your weight is as much about learning to manage your food intake as it is learning to manage your emotions. You can't master one without the other. This book is called *The Best Diet Begins in Your Mind* for a reason. When your mind is on board, your body will follow.

This book is for you if

- you are a yo-yo dieter—having gained and lost the same pounds time and time again and want to break that cycle;
- you start the day with the best of intentions only to slip off your diet before noon because something or

someone interferes, even though you really want to stay the course;

- you are worried you'll never lose weight and don't know what to do;
- you are you feeling discouraged about any future weight-loss efforts you might undertake because of repeated failures in the past;
- you realize that your emotions are getting in the way of sticking to your food and exercise plans; or
- you are you ready to eliminate the emotional obstacles that may be sabotaging your weight-loss goals once and for all.

It doesn't matter if you are a man or a woman, five pounds overweight or a hundred pounds overweight. It doesn't matter if you have been struggling with your weight all your life or if you've gained weight recently. What matters is that you are here now and are willing to address your weight issues from a new perspective.

Remember—this is not a quick weight-loss scheme. The way you have been living so far has kept your body and your weight where it is now. To change your weight and your body for good, you will need to learn to live your life in a way that supports your new svelte figure. This means you will need to learn to eat differently, exercise differently, and manage your emotional life differently. This book addresses the third part of that equation.

Use this book with any food plan that meets your nutritional needs and is flexible enough for you to follow for the rest of your life. A diet that tells you to eliminate a particular food group or to eat only certain foods at certain times is unlikely to be one that you can embrace for the next forty or fifty years. Work with a nutritionist or reputable weight-loss program to find a plan that will work for you for the long haul.

Or you may choose not to follow a formal food plan as you begin this journey. That's fine with me. Some people find that, once they get their emotional lives in order, the food falls into place. Do what feels right for you.

As for exercise, the same holds true. Find a form of exercise that is appropriate for your body and that you enjoy so that you will participate in it for years to come. Be creative. Vary your routine, and have some fun. Exercise, in whatever form works for you, needs to be a part of your lifestyle from this moment forward. If you are not sure where to start, contact a personal trainer, visit your local Y, or search the Internet for ideas.

Once you have your food plan and exercise plan set up, you are ready to begin. Use this book as an adjunct to your dieting and exercise efforts. Rely on it to help you navigate the emotional obstacles that will inevitably fall in your path. Expect them. Prepare for them. Manage them. Doing so will set you on your way to achieving your goal—permanent weight loss.

We will begin with a discussion of the difference between physical and emotional hunger. Once you master the difference, you will find it easier to stick to your designated plan.

Then we will address each of the eight emotional obstacles that may sabotage your dieting efforts. Each emotion will be clearly defined so you can identify it operating in your life. You will learn what they are, how they operate, and what you can do to manage them. You will be given actions you can take to deal with the emotional obstacle so you no longer have to eat over it.

Through the book you will find "About Me" sections.

Use them to jot down your insights, aha moments, and other thoughts you may have about what you just read or what you may have learned about yourself. These notes will prove to be very valuable as you move toward your ideal weight.

Each chapter ends with an "Action Plan" section, where you can describe what you will do in the face of that emotion. Then transfer your notes to a comprehensive action plan, "My Emotional Obstacles Action Plan," found at the end of the book. This way you'll have everything you need in one place.

You will also find advice on how to achieve your ideal weight and how to use a variety of tools, including your imagination, to help you succeed.

In time, you will find that emotions are merely energy in your body that needs acknowledgment and expression. If you give yourself permission to feel your feelings, you will find that they provide valuable information about your life, your self, and your relationships.

By addressing your emotional life, you will find it is easier to stay on your plan, and remaining on your plan will lead to the results you seek. So as you move forward with this material, allow yourself to be with your emotions. You'll be happy you did. Now, get to work.

Here's to your good health, physical and emotional, and to your ideal body weight—whatever it may be.

CHAPTER ONE

Physical versus Emotional Hunger

We've all been hungry. You know that gnawing feeling in your gut that tells you it's time to eat. Or is it? Are you truly hungry, or would you just like to eat something? True hunger, the kind that alerts you to the physiological needs of your body, is physical in nature. The hunger that leads to just wanting to eat is emotional. A common problem among people trying to lose weight is the inability to distinguish between these two hungers. Physical hunger is real hunger. It's your body's message to your mind that it (your body) needs fuel to function. Physical hunger is biological. It is the primal survival mechanism that keeps us alive. If you fail to eat when you are physically hungry, you deprive your body of the nutrients it needs to keep going. Eventually, it ceases to function, and you die. If you tune into your physical hunger and eat according to its message, you will eat what your body needs—no more, no less. Doing so will keep your body humming along in a fashion that is best for you and at a weight that is right for you.

Emotional hunger is pseudohunger. It has nothing to do with physical survival. Emotional hunger is your mind's desire to eat when you are feeling an uncomfortable emotion. It is your mind's way of coping with that emotion and getting it to go away. Since this type of hunger is not related to your body's physical needs, it creates a scenario for excess calories to be consumed, which, of course, lead inevitably to weight gain (or, if you are dieting, to a failure to lose weight).

The key to dealing with emotional hunger is learning to identify the emotion you are feeling and to address it in a constructive, healthy manner. There is no reason to eat over an emotion, because emotions have nothing to do with food.

So how do you tell if you are physically or emotionally hungry? Here are some questions to help you out. Answer yes or no to each one the next time you find yourself wanting to eat something:

Are You Physically Hungry?

1. Have I eaten in the past two to three hours?
2. Did what I last ate fill me up?
3. Am I willing to eat a piece of fruit or some vegetables to satisfy my hunger?
4. Is my stomach growling?
5. Am I feeling a bit light-headed?
6. Can I no longer concentrate on what I am doing because I want/need to eat?
7. Do I have a slight headache?
8. Do I feel shaky?
9. Am I feeling groggy?
10. Is my mind starting to get a bit foggy?

You can recognize physical hunger by its cues. For most people, those cues include the sensations described in questions 4 through 10. You may have other signals, such as an enhanced sense of smell or mouth watering. Get to know yourself so you are clear on how your body tells you when it needs food. Then, when you are physically hungry, eat something. Prepare yourself a healthy meal or snack in accordance with your food plan, set the table, sit down, and enjoy.

Since the focus of this book is on the emotional aspects of eating, I won't be addressing nutrition. So if you need assistance in knowing what a healthy snack or meal might look like, you can contact the Academy of Nutrition and Dietetics (www.eatright.org) for a referral to a registered dietitian in your area.

On the other hand, if you are not physically hungry and still want to eat, your emotions are triggering your desire. Answer the next ten questions to see if you are emotionally hungry.

Are You Emotionally Hungry?

1. Is it mealtime (so it's time to eat)?
2. Do I need a little pick-me-up to keep going because I am feeling tired?
3. Am I bored and eating something would give me something to do?
4. Do I have an empty feeling inside that needs to be filled up right now?
5. Am I angry and don't know how/what to do with the anger?
6. Am I feeling lonely and a big bowl of ice cream would make me feel better?
7. Am I sad about something and a bar of chocolate sounds good right about now?
8. Do I feel deprived in any area of my life and refuse to deny myself when it comes to what I am going to eat?

9. Do I want to throw in the towel on my dieting efforts and eat whatever I want because it doesn't matter anyway?
10. Am I feeling worried or stressed-out and think eating would help calm me down?

If you recognize that your desire to eat is emotional rather than physical, you are at a crossroads. This moment is the time you can take control of your eating and get on the path to permanent weight loss. Now you have the chance to exercise *choice.*

Sure, you can eat if you want to. In fact, in my psychotherapy and coaching practices, I never tell my patients not to eat. But I do educate them that they have a choice. You can choose to eat, or you can choose to address the emotional trigger. The more times you choose to address the emotional trigger directly rather than "eat over it," the less excess calories you will consume—and, well, you do the math. This book will help you if you choose to address your emotional issues directly. Let me show you how.

About Me

Use this space to record what you know about your own body's mechanism for showing physical hunger. Pay attention to the physical sensations that accompany your genuine need to eat. The more you focus on this, the easier it will get to recognize.

_____

_____

_____

_____

CHAPTER TWO

Why We Overeat: Soothing with Food

I'm going to guess that, if you are reading this book, you are an intelligent person who is successful in many aspects of life. So why not this one? Why, after all the diets you've been on, are you still carrying more weight than you want? Why, with all the knowledge you have about food, exercise, and portion control, are you still struggling? My answer is very simple—along the way, you learned to use food to soothe yourself. It may have started with your mother offering you a cookie when you skinned your knee or an ice cream cone after a fight with your best friend. You may have continued the pattern yourself with a pint of Ben & Jerry's after a breakup or a couple of tacos on your way home after a hard day's work. Whatever the scenario, along the way, food became your medicine. And it worked. It made you feel better—at least momentarily.

Food works to help you feel better for several reasons, but there are three main reasons that we will focus on. First, food works to change how you feel because food affects our bodies' biochemistry. Without getting too scientific, it's important to understand some of the physiological effects of food on our bodies and our brains.

Food is a substance. As a substance, it acts upon our bodies to produce certain results. The body breaks down food into chemicals, and the blood carries these chemicals throughout our bodies. The brain also contains chemicals that are affected by what they detect in the blood. These brain chemicals are known as neurotransmitters and are responsible for all sorts of experiences in our bodies. The brain is designed to make adjustments to our bodies' chemical processes based on what it detects. Too much or too little of a substance will affect our emotions.

One such neurotransmitter is called dopamine. It is responsible for our feeling pleasure. When we eat, the dopamine receptors in our brain are activated, and as a consequence, we feel pleasure. Thus, we learn to associate food with pleasure.

Some foods also affect the levels of another neurotransmitter we have in our bodies called serotonin. Serotonin is known as a "feel-good" neurotransmitter; too little of it, and we feel depressed. Drugs like Prozac, which is classified as an SSRI (selective serotonin reuptake inhibitor), are used to treat depression because they affect the levels of serotonin circulating in our brains. Food can do a similar thing. Food can increase the amount of serotonin we have and, consequently, lift our spirits.

The second reason food works to help you feel better is it takes our minds off our troubles—at least for a while. Food is a fabulous distractor. Buying it, preparing it, serving it, and cleaning up afterward are all effective ways to take us out of where we are and into something different. Suddenly, we are no longer thinking about our difficult boss or the traffic on the freeway. No, now are minds are filled with thoughts of cheesy pizzas and garlic rolls. Then, if you factor in the remorse we feel after eating and the subsequent plotting of our next diet (or binge), you can start to see how focusing your attention on food and its related activities can easily remove you from your present-day woes.

A third reason food "works" is that it is a conditioned response. Do you remember Pavlov and his famous experiments with dogs? Pavlov noticed that the dogs in his experiments would salivate whenever he gave them meat. It was an automatic response. He wondered if he could get them to salivate at other times as well. To test this, Pavlov rang a bell at the same time as he presented the dogs with the meat. The dogs naturally salivated in response to the meat. After a while, Pavlov stopped giving the dogs meat when he rang the bell. Much to his delight, the dogs salivated anyway. In other words, they learned to salivate just to the sound of the bell. The dogs made an association between the bell and the meat, such that salivating to the sound of the bell had become an automatic response. In this experiment, Pavlov taught us that, when we associate unrelated stimuli (the bell and the meat) together, a previously neutral stimulus (the bell) becomes activating (it causes salivation.)

What does this mean for you and your relationships to food? Simple. Over time, you have associated food with feeling good. Food by itself is neutral, but after a lifetime of treating yourself to sweets after a hard day or eating a bag of chips on the couch watching *CSI*, you have learned to associate food with these events. Turning to food becomes your automatic response to particular situations. Think about it for a second. If I say birthday, you say … cake. If I say Valentine's Day, you say … chocolate. If I say your team won the softball game, you say … burgers and fries. Do you get the picture?

Think about your relationship with food and how you use it to soothe away your emotional pain. Do you notice a psychological change or physiological change after you eat something? Is eating the primary tool you use for avoiding unpleasant situations or feelings? Is your eating a learned behavior? A habit? Record your thoughts here. Refer back to them at a later time to see what has changed and what still needs improvement.

About Me

_____

_____

_____

_____

_____

_____

_____

_____

_____

_____

_____

_____

_____

_____

_____

_____

_____

_____

_____

_____

_____

_____

_____

_____

_____

_____

_____

_____

_____

_____

_____

_____

_____

_____

_____

_____

_____

_____

_____

_____

_____

_____

_____

_____

_____

_____

_____

_____

_____

_____

_____

_____

Now let's move onto "the Eight Emotional Obstacles" and what you can do about them.

CHAPTER THREE

The Eight Emotional Obstacles: An Overview

To be sure, we can feel a lot of different emotions at any given time. Some of those emotions are based in sadness, others in fear, and some in joy. In an attempt to simplify the idea that we eat either because of physical hunger or emotional hunger, I have identified the eight emotions that I have seen my patients eat in response to most often.

The eight emotional obstacles I have observed, and which will be the basis for the rest of this book, are:

1. Anger
2. Boredom and emptiness
3. Deprivation
4. Fear and anxiety
5. Hopelessness
6. Loneliness
7. Sadness and depression
8. Stress and tension

You may notice that these are the emotions that are based on sadness and fear. I have not included emotions that are based in joy, such as happiness, excitement, and anticipation. Yes, people do eat over those emotions. Just think celebratory dinners, holidays, and birthdays as examples. The reason I did not include them is that, in my experience, people feel "negative" emotions more often and therefore eat in response to those emotions more frequently than the "positive" ones.

Of course, it is possible that your celebratory dinners and holiday plans are not filled with joy at all. It is common for such situations to be fraught with negative emotions and painful experiences. In fact, I make it a habit not to take vacation during the Christmas season so I can be available for my patients if there is a crisis. If this is true for you, I think you will find the suggestions presented in this book to be most helpful.

One more comment about "positive" emotions and overeating before we move on. For many people, feeling a positive emotion is uncomfortable, and it is this discomfort that leads to the excess eating. You may be asking why feeling good would be uncomfortable. Well, the answer is different for different people, but some of the reasons include (1) they feel undeserving of the good that is happening, (2) they feel anxious that the good won't last, (3) they are not used to the feeling and its strangeness is unnerving, and (4) the feeling inside them feels odd and they want it to go away. Does any of this sound like you? If it does, you can apply what you learn about dealing with negative emotions to the positive ones.

But remember, anytime you eat in response to an emotion—be it positive or negative—you are eating for emotional reasons and are adding excess calories to your daily intake, leading to extra unwanted weight. Next time you are feeling good and want to celebrate, pick an activity that brings you joy without extra calories. For example, call a friend, go for a walk in a new place, ride your bike, or see a movie.

To figure out if the "Eight Emotional Obstacles" are getting in the way of your permanent weight-loss goal, begin by asking yourself these revealing questions:

> *Anger* – Are you feeling mad about something or at someone? Is it hard for you to express those feelings? Do you ever find yourself eating those feeling down?

> *Boredom and emptiness* – Do you have times in your day, week, or life when you feel there is nothing to do, no one to be with, or nowhere to go? Do you fill it with food or food-related activities such as shopping, cooking, watching the food network, or reading cookbooks? Or do you feel as if you have a huge hole inside of you? Have you tried to fill that hole, but it never fills up? Does it feel as if there isn't enough food in the world to make you feel full?

> *Deprivation* – Are there any areas in your life where you feel as if you do not have what you really want? If you want something, do you have to have it now? If someone tells you you can't eat something, does that make you want it even more?

> *Fear and anxiety* – Does the world frighten you? Are there things you'd like to do but

are afraid to try? Does eating ever calm you down or give you courage?

Hopelessness – Have you given up on yourself, your life, and your weight-loss efforts? Do you feel as if there is no reason to try again because you always fail? Do you feel as if you might as well eat because nothing else works?

Loneliness – Are you feeling like you don't have enough friends, the right relationship, or a close confidant? Are you in the wrong relationship, the wrong friendship, or the wrong marriage? Do you ever feel that food is your only friend?

Sadness and depression – Is your heart broken? Did you suffer a loss of some kind? Does eating something sweet lift your spirits?

Stress and tension – Are you feeling uptight, burned-out, or worried? Does a tub of ice cream soothe your nerves at the end of a long day?

So, what did you notice? If you answered yes to any of these questions, you may be eating for emotional reasons. If you are, you are in the right place. The rest of this book will teach you to address these emotional reasons by learning to manage them in healthy, constructive ways. As you do, you will watch yourself achieve your weight-loss goals.

About Me

Before you move on, jot down some thoughts about where you are and what you have learned so far. Include any goals or ideas you want to keep in mind as you proceed. And, if any of the eight emotional obstacles are a particular trigger for you, make note of that as well. The more you know about yourself, the more you will get from this journey.

_____

_____

_____

_____

_____

_____

_____

_____

_____

_____

_____

_____

_____

_____

_____

_____

_____

_____

_____

_____

_____

_____

_____

CHAPTER FOUR

Anger

I've listed anger as the first emotional obstacle to address, not just because it starts with *A* but because, in my experience, anger is a huge saboteur of people's weight-loss efforts. Let's take a look at anger—what it is, how it feels, what it looks like, and what you can do about it.

What Is Anger?

According to the American Psychological Association (www.apa.org), anger is a normal emotion we all experience, characterized by animosity toward someone or something we feel has intentionally done us wrong. It is an intense emotion that comes from a belief that we have been unfairly treated. Of course, anger can happen in degrees; it can range from a mere annoyance to outright rage.

Whether it is a nuisance or a tantrum, for many, anger is an emotion to be feared and avoided. Some people go to great lengths not to express their anger because they are afraid of it. They are afraid that, if they allow their anger to emerge, it will overwhelm them. They are afraid of what they might do or say because of their anger. In an effort to avoid anger, many "eat it away." They suppress angry feelings with food, burying it deep within their bodies so they don't have to feel it, face it, or deal with it.

However, anger can be a good thing. It can give you a way to express negative feelings, for example, or motivate you to find solutions to problems. Nevertheless, excessive anger can cause problems that can harm your physical and mental health. It's when anger gets out of hand that it can cause problems in a person's life.

How Does Anger Feel?

Some physical manifestations of anger include a clenched jaw, a stiffening of the body, trembling, and even headaches and stomachaches. Some people literally get hot under the collar. Their body temperatures rise, and they get red in the face. Some sweat.

The psychological manifestations of anger can include swearing, thoughts of revenge, obsessional thinking, and fear.

The above descriptions of anger are by no means the only manifestations. Anger is experienced uniquely by each individual. Take some time now to think about how you experience anger? What does it feel like in your body? In your mind? Do you even experience anger? Is it okay to do so? In a little bit, you will read about Debbie, a person who didn't allow herself to get angry.

What Makes You Angry?

As mentioned above, anger can happen as a matter of degrees. You may be annoyed by a parking ticket or irritable because you are tired. At the other end, you may be totally enraged because a competitor outbid you on a contract.

The degrees of anger may be categorized as follows:

- annoyance
- frustration
- irritation
- resentment
- antagonism
- fury
- wrath
- rage

You can see the range from mild to vicious. Look these descriptions over. Have you ever felt them? If yes, when? What were the circumstances?

During a lecture I gave at a local university, I asked the students to make a list of things that make them angry. Here's their list. Does this list look like your list?

- breakup of a relationship
- failed course when they tried hard
- hot temperatures
- final exams given in multiple classes on the same day
- traffic
- long lines
- inconsiderate drivers
- unhelpful salespeople
- latecomers
- cancellations
- loud noises
- people in their space
- sloppy roommates
- unreturned texts and phone calls

What makes you angry? You can tell from my students' responses that the situations that provoked their anger are around school and relationships. What about you? And how angry do you get? Is your anger proportionate to its cause? For instance, going ballistic over a twenty-five-dollar parking ticket is a bit over the top. Understanding the cause and extent of your anger will help you find different ways of managing it.

People feel anger for all sorts of reasons. In my experience, one reason people get angry is that they feel as if they have not been treated fairly. For example, you've worked hard for a promotion and your coworker gets the job instead. Or you've been in line at the grocery store for five minutes when another cashier opens up and takes a customer standing behind you. Sound familiar?

Another reason people get angry is that they feel as if they are not being heard or are being disregarded. For example, you've asked your husband several times to take the garbage to the curb and the cans are still in the driveway. Or you'd prefer Chinese food before the movies and your friends insist on Italian.

Furthermore, anger can flare up if you are tired, frustrated, or impatient. These states of mind make it harder to cope with whatever you are facing and can leave you feeling angry.

In my opinion, anger is a healthy emotion. If we pay attention, it tells us that something is wrong and needs our consideration. Sometimes, what is wrong is the circumstance. Other times, what is wrong is how we are dealing with that circumstance. Either way, acknowledging your anger is healthy and can lead to less overeating.

What Can You Do When You Feel Angry?

Anger is not an emotion to be feared. It is an emotion to be expressed. If you are uncomfortable feeling anger or have been taught that it is not okay to be angry, you may eat it away. What do I mean by that? Well, you may attempt to squash your angry feelings with food by eating until you are numb. There is anecdotal evidence that angry people eat crunchy food to calm themselves down. There is something about biting down hard on chips, for example, that is very satisfying.

A healthy expression of anger is a vital skill that everyone can learn. The key is to release it without being aggressive. Also, try to address your anger in the moment it occurs rather than let it fester and grow by holding onto it.

Here are some steps for expressing your anger in a way that helps rather than hurts you:

Step One: Recognize that you are angry.

Step Two: Identify what/who is making you angry.

Step Three: Give yourself permission to be angry.

Step Four: Pick a safe way to express your anger. For example:

- Use assertive language to say what you need to say to the person who has angered you.
- If expressing your anger directly to the person who angered you is not possible or too scary, you can express your anger in other ways, such as telling a therapist, writing about in a journal

or unmailed letter, or confiding in a trusted friend.

- Some more creative expressions of anger include writing the name of the person or situation that angers you on the sole of your shoe and stomping around.
- Write the offending name or situation on a dozen raw eggs and break them against the shower wall.
- Cry.
- Yell into a pillow.
- Hit your mattress with a tennis racket.
- Physically release your anger by exercising, running, walking, hitting tennis balls, or shooting baskets.

Step Five: Express it.

(*Note*: If you ever feel as if your anger is getting out of hand or is uncontrollable, please get professional help. My first career was as a lawyer, and in those years, I saw too many people get into too much trouble because of unbridled anger. Trust me; you don't want to end up in jail, divorce court, or worse because of your temper. A psychologist trained in anger management is an excellent resource. You can contact the American Psychological Association [www.apa.org] or your local psychological organization for referrals.)

Take a look at how Debbie dealt with her angry. See what you can learn about yourself.

* * * * *

Debbie, a Case Study of Anger

If you met Debbie, you'd really like her. A petite blond with green eyes and the sweetest southern accent this side of the Mississippi, Debbie was forty-four years old when she came to me about her weight. Standing only five foot one, Debbie weighed close to 280 pounds. A married mother of two, Debbie worked part-time in an accountant's office as a bookkeeper. Oh, did I mention, the accountant was Stan, her husband of eighteen years? When Debbie married Stan, her weight was healthy, about 150 pounds less than when we met. As she told me about her weight history and eating habits, I couldn't figure out why she had gained so much weight. She reported making good choices and eating healthy portions.

It wasn't until I asked her about her relationship with Stan that I started to grasp the situation. Stan is a difficult man, very critical and demeaning. At work, he would insult her in front of the other employees. At home, he would criticize her cooking, housekeeping, and child-rearing practices. From my point of view, Stan was emotionally abusive. From Debbie's point of view, Stan was just being Stan.

When I asked her how she felt about how Stan treated her and if it ever made her angry, she told me that Southern women don't get angry. It wasn't proper. Now I understood the problem. Instead of acknowledging her angry feelings about how she was being treated, she unknowingly ate them down. The more Stan attacked her, the more she ate.

I invited Debbie into a psychotherapy group with other women. Over time, they "educated" her that Stan's treatment of her was not okay and "taught" her to identify and feel anger. As Debbie learned to express her anger in healthy and constructive ways, she began to eat less, and slowly over time, her excess weight came off. She and Stan are still married, but they have a different kind of marriage. She no longer tolerates his belittling remarks and tells him so, and she works part-time somewhere else.

* * * * *

Have you had to deal with a situation like this one? How has anger affected your food intake? Which healthy expression of anger are you willing to try the next time you feel angry? Write your thoughts here.

About Me

_____

_____

_____

_____

_____

_____

_____

_____

_____

_____

_____

_____

_____

_____

_____

_____

_____

_____

_____

_____

_____

_____

_____

_____

_____

_____

Now that you have an idea of what *anger* is and the role it may play in your eating habits, it's time to make a plan for what you will do to deal with angry feelings the next time they show up. Use the space below to write down your ideas and then transfer your ideas to the "My Emotional Obstacles Action Plan" in the back of the book. In that action plan, you will detail all your strategies for overcoming your emotional obstacles to permanent weight loss. Refer to it often to help you get through the tough times.

Dealing with My Anger Action Plan

The strategies I can employ to deal with *anger* instead of eating are:

1.

2.

3.

4.

5.

Boredom and Emptiness

How are you doing so far? I hope that you found the discussion on anger instructive and that you have some idea of the process I am teaching you—to identify what you are feeling, to understand why you are feeling it, and to do something other than eating to deal with it.

In this chapter, we will look at another emotion (actually two versions of one emotion) to move you further along in your journey to your ideal weight.

This may be my "favorite" emotional obstacle, if it is possible to have a favorite. The reason I call it my favorite is that I think this is the one that may be the easiest to address. But first, a quick word about boredom. Did you know that boredom can actually be an expression of anger? It can.

Most people think of boredom as having nothing to do, and much of the time, that is exactly what it is. But boredom can also be an indirect way of expressing anger. Sometimes, when you are angry about something but cannot express it, you may feel "bored." Or you may find yourself withdrawn and isolated and, as a result, feel bored because you have nothing to do and no one to be with. But the actual cause is unexpressed anger.

Think about it. Have you ever found yourself saying to yourself, "I'm bored; I don't want to do this anymore," when you are in the middle of a task you don't like to do? If so, your "boredom" might actually be anger at having to do the task in the first place. Remember, anger can happen in degrees. So an unrecognized feeling of frustration, for example, can show up as boredom.

My client Todd was in this afternoon, and he really demonstrated this idea. Todd is forty-seven, newly single and miserable. He came in complaining that he spent the entire weekend home with nothing to do. He went on for quite a while about how he channel surfed and ate pizza all day long. When I asked how he felt, all he could say was he was bored. Finally, I asked him about his ex-fiancée. At first, he refused to talk about her.

With a little cajoling, he started to open up about how wonderful she was and how he missed her. I pushed a bit more, and finally, he got angry. At last, he talked about how mad he was about her breaking off their engagement. Todd wasn't bored this weekend; he was angry. But he didn't know it, so he watched TV and ate pizza.

If this is the case for you, go back to the last chapter on anger and use the ideas there to help yourself out. If not, let's move on.

What Is Boredom?

At their cores, boredom and emptiness are similar, but there is an important difference between them we will be exploring. Boredom is experienced on the outside, while emptiness is experienced on the inside. Let me explain.

Boredom (when it isn't anger) occurs because we are feeling under-stimulated. You know that feeling when you are wandering around looking for something to do, read, or watch on TV and nothing is satisfying. The danger comes when that hunt for something to do leads to the refrigerator. You open the fridge and look inside. Nothing. So you wander some more. Then you look again. This time, you spot some leftover cake or pasta and you dig in. For a while, you are busy—busy eating, busy cleaning up, busy feeling badly about what you just did. Time spent. Day over.

What Is Emptiness?

Emptiness, on the other hand, happens when your life is missing key pieces. Key pieces are those things that make your life full and exciting, such as satisfying relationships and interesting hobbies,

To determine if you might be suffering from emptiness, ask yourself these questions:

- Do you find yourself spending weekend after weekend doing nothing more than running errands and watching television?
- As a consequence, do your errands include visits to your favorite fast-food joint or convenience store for a hefty supply of snacks?
- And do you spend the rest of your time lying on the couch noshing on the treats you brought home?
- Is your job uninteresting? Is it just a job rather than a career or a calling?
- Do you look for reasons to slip away from your desk and head to the break room for the donuts and bagels that are usually there?
- Is the highlight of your workday lunch?

These are all examples of the kinds of emptiness that infiltrate people's lives and leave them seeking comfort in food.

Another way that emptiness could be playing a role is if you are using food and its accompanying behaviors to fill in your life with activity. It takes a lot of time to plan, shop, cook, eat, clean up, and start over. It also takes a lot of time to pick a diet, start a diet, quit a diet, and start again. Busy. Busy. Busy. I know many people for whom that was the real purpose dieting and eating played in their lives. You will meet one of those people in a moment. Her name is Holly, and her story is below.

What Do Your Boredom and Emptiness Feelings Look Like?

Before you meet Holly, let's take some time to consider what boredom and emptiness look like and the roles they play in your weight-loss and eating history. To begin with, which of these feels more relevant to you and your experiences? Or do both play a part?

Here are some ways to recognize boredom:

- You read the same paragraph several times without comprehension.
- You pass in front of the fridge wondering if there is anything to eat.
- You check your e-mail repeatedly.
- You say to yourself, "I have nothing to do."

Here are some ways to recognize emptiness:

- You envy things your friends have.
- Certain commercials make you cry.

- You avoid events such as weddings or reunions.
- You say to yourself, "I don't have what I want."

When you feel bored, do you eat? Do you cook? Do you plan your next diet? If yes, then these are ways that boredom plays a role in your weight issues.

You may also eat to feel full even though you have already eaten a regular-size meal. You may spend your Saturday afternoons and evenings with food shopping, cooking, and then eating in front of the TV. Or you may call the pizza delivery guy several times a week so that you have someone to talk to, if only for a few moments. These are all examples of how emptiness might affect your food habits.

Take a moment to think about your life and how boredom and emptiness may have sabotaged your dieting efforts.

What Can You Do When You Feel Bored or Empty?

If your boredom is caused by a lack of interesting activities or because you are feeling under-stimulated and restless and have lots of time on your hands, your best strategy will be to add interests and activities—both external and internal—to your life. Here are some ideas to get you started.

- Call a friend, and go to the movies.
- Make new friends by joining a sports team or charitable organization.
- Try a new hobby.
- Take a class through your local adult education program.
- Try a new sport.
- Read the latest best seller.
- Exercise.

- Join a church or synagogue.
- Pray.
- Meditate.
- Join a Bible study class.
- Attend spirituality meetings.
- Develop a spiritual practice.

If your boredom is actually an indirect expression of anger, remember to review Chapter Four on anger and see if you can find a way to release your angry feelings. If you can, I suspect your feelings of boredom will go away.

If the emotion you are feeling is emptiness rather than boredom, the real key will be to take a cold, hard look at what is missing from your life and then take steps to bring it in.

Similar to the steps for expressing anger, here's how to begin dealing with your boredom and emptiness:

Step One: Recognize that you are bored or empty.

Step Two: Identify why you are feeling bored or empty.

Step Three: Give yourself permission to be bored or empty.

Step Four: Pick a way to relieve your boredom or emptiness from the list above or think of something new.

Step Five: Do it now.

Now let's meet another patient of mine, Caitlin, who was eating out of boredom. You may recognize yourself in her story. I hope you do. She had a very happy ending. I wish the same for you.

* * * * *

Caitlin, a Case Study of Boredom

From time to time, I work with a patient for whom I worry that psychotherapy is failing. As hard as I try to help this patient improve the quality of his or her life, nothing happens. I am reminded of sage words from a mentor of mine who told me that, when I am working harder than the patient is to change her life, I am doing too much. That is how I felt about Caitlin.

Week after week she would come in complaining about her weight, complaining about her life, complaining that she was "bored to death." And week after week, session after session, I would talk with her about her unwillingness to do anything different—her resistance to helping herself. I explained that understanding why you are the way you are is very valuable, and equally valuable is applying what you have learned from therapy to build a better life. She eventually agreed with what I said and promised to try.

We came up with a plan for her to pick one new event, class, or activity to attend during the week. And she did, but nothing seemed to make a difference. She would still complain of being bored and eat her way through the hours she spent at home—until she discovered jewelry making. On a whim, she signed up for a one-day bead-stringing class at our local community college. As she said, she had nothing to lose. She went to the class and loved it. She saw that she could be creative and innovative, and it was fun.

This first class turned into a series. The series eventually turned into a full-blown hobby. Now Caitlin spends her free time beading jewelry for friends and for sale. She attends workshops and classes and goes to arts and crafts shows. Her boredom no longer exists. She found an interest that totally occupies her. Now she is so busy she forgets to eat. Given that she no longer spends countless hours at home eating because she has nothing else to do, Caitlin is on her way to permanent weight loss.

* * * * *

And you? What activities or hobbies can you enjoy that would relieve boredom?

About Me

_____

_____

_____

_____

_____

_____

_____

_____

_____

_____

_____

_____

_____

_____

_____

_____

Please meet Holly. Her story about emptiness is quite moving.

* * * * * *

Holly, a Case Study of Emptiness

Holly came to me weighing over three hundred pounds at the age of twenty-eight. She was an attractive woman with wavy, black hair and big, brown eyes. She had a wonderful sense of humor and a quick wit. I always looked forward to our sessions because she was truly a delight to be with. By day, Holly was a lawyer, a stressful job to say the least. She worked in a small, four-person law firm specializing in landlord-tenant issues. She spent a lot of time in court pursuing evictions. The work was not especially interesting to Holly, but as she would always say, "It pays the bills."

Holly comes from a long line of lawyers. Her grandmother was the first woman to graduate from her law school. Her mother was on law review. Holly did okay in law school but was not, by her own admission, a "star."

Besides going to her job, Holly's life revolved around food. Reading cookbooks and cooking magazines was her hobby. She loved the Food Network and would come in week after week telling me about this recipe or that, which was featured on one of the shows. From time to time, she would bring me samples of what she had cooked over the weekend, even though I had a strict "no food in session" policy.

We spent countless hours discussing why she kept bringing me food until she had an epiphany. Food was her life—her whole life. She had nothing else going on. She hadn't noticed it before because she was so busy with her cooking shows and recipe testing. When she came to this realization, she broke down and cried. She cried for the career she didn't enjoy, the family of her own she didn't have, and the lost years she'd spent focused on food.

From that point on, our work become about identifying what would give Holly the life she really wanted. Slowly but surely, she added pieces in. First, she changed jobs. She was more interested in adoption law than evictions. She joined a family law firm and built up a successful practice. In the course of doing that, she met a hard-to-place child and fell in love. It took a little time, but eventually, Holly adopted her. Now she had her own family.

Her life went from being focused on food to being focused on her daughter and her career. What happened to Holly's weight after all of this? You guessed it—it came off. She became so busy with a life that was fulfilling she didn't need to fill herself up with empty calories anymore. She turned to cooking healthy recipes when she had time, and the weight took care of itself.

* * * * *

Do you cook? Is there something about this story that inspires you? What can you do to fill in the emptiness? Write your thoughts here.

About Me

_____

_____

_____

_____

_____

_____

_____

_____

_____

_____

_____

_____

_____

_____

_____

_____

_____

_____

_____

_____

_____

_____

_____

_____

_____

_____

_____

_____

_____

_____

_____

_____

Now that you have an idea of what *boredom* and *emptiness* are and the role they may play in your eating habits, it's time to make a plan for what you will do to deal with these feelings the next time you feel them. Use the space below to write down your ideas and then transfer your ideas to the

"My Emotional Obstacles Action Plan" in the back of the book. Remember, that action plan will be your go-to guide for coping with difficult situations.

Dealing with My Boredom Action Plan

The strategies I can employ to deal with *boredom* instead of eating are:

1.

2.

3.

4.

5.

Dealing with My Emptiness Action Plan

The strategies I can employ to deal with *emptiness* instead of eating are:

1.

2.

3.

4.

5.

CHAPTER SIX

Deprivation

Now we will look at an emotion that, for many, can be very painful and that is the root of much emotional eating. Like in the previous chapter on boredom and emptiness, in this chapter, we will look at two sides of one emotion. This time our focus is on deprivation—food deprivation and loss deprivation.

What Is Deprivation?

When I ask people to tell me which emotions they believe cause people to overeat, they rarely say "deprivation." And yet, I find it to be a major reason for emotional overeating. From my experience, there are two kinds of deprivations operating when it comes to food and eating.

The first kind of deprivation is based on what people are "allowed" or "not allowed" to eat on their food plans. If, for example, you are on a low-fat diet, you may feel deprived of full-fat flavors, like ice cream or cheese. This sense of deprivation can lead you to overeat to make up for the things you perceive to be missing. I call this "food deprivation.

The second kind of deprivation comes from a sense of

loss in one's life. For example, let's say your father left your family when you were a child. You may be feeling deprived of having a father figure or deprived of having a happy, secure childhood. Later in life, you may eat to fill the void the loss created. I've noticed that most people who do this don't even realize they are doing so until they come into therapy and the connection is shown to them. I call this "loss deprivation."

Loss deprivation can also show up as a sense of something missing in the here and now. As an example, let's consider a patient of mine who miscarried a child in the last trimester of her pregnancy. After that loss, she was devastated. When I met her two years later, she was sixty-five pounds overweight—the exact amount of weight she'd been carrying when she was pregnant. In therapy, she was able to make the connection between her weight and her loss. As she mourned her loss, the weight came off.

How Does Deprivation Feel?

If your deprivation is food deprivation caused by the food plan you have chosen, rethink it. A successful food plan takes into account all the food available to you but in appropriate quantities. Choose a plan that includes your favorite foods from time to time. By giving yourself permission to eat the foods you enjoy, you can prevent a binge.

Without that permission, food deprivation can feel like intense cravings and turn into obsessive thinking about the "forbidden" food. For example, if I tell you that you can never eat pie again, all you are going to want to eat is pie.

Another version of this is what I call "last-supper" eating. The night before a diet that excludes certain foods can lead to an all-night pig-out of the foods you fear you will never eat again.

Those who eat because they are experiencing loss deprivation describe their deprivation as an ache. They describe a pain within their gut or they say, "It hurts in my bones." It is a physical sensation that has no physical cause. The cause of the discomfort is emotional. And, as with any other emotional pain, the way to deal with it is at its source. Shortly, you'll meet Linda, who was experiencing a profound sense of deprivation and was able to overcome it by recognizing it and addressing it directly.

What Does Your Deprivation Look Like?

Now it's your turn. Are you struggling with food deprivation or loss deprivation or both? To understand how deprivation may present an emotional obstacle to your weight-loss efforts, ask yourself these questions:

Food Deprivation:
- Does my food plan eliminate any food groups?
  - If yes, how do I feel about that food group?
  - Do I miss it?
- Does my food plan restrict my choices in anyway?
  - If yes, how do I feel about those restrictions?
  - Do I miss the foods that are restricted?
- Am I experiencing any cravings?
  - If yes, what for and when?
  - What would happen if gave into those cravings?
- Is my mind filled with about food?
  - If yes, which foods?
  - Why?
  - How often do I have those thoughts?
  - When do I have them?

- If I am not following a food plan, am I allowing myself to eat from all food groups?
  - If not, why not?
- If I am not following a food plan am I avoiding any particular foods?
  - If yes, why?
  - What would happen if I included them?

Loss Deprivation

Now let's take a look at what might be missing from your life. Here we are thinking about things such as relationships, satisfying work, interesting hobbies, spiritual connections, and a fulfilling social life. If you had something or someone in your life that is now gone, I call that "real" deprivation. If there is something you wish for, I call that "imaginary" deprivation. Keeping these ideas in mind, answer the following questions:

- Are you deprived of anything in your life?
- If yes, what is it?
- Is what you are deprived of real or imaginary?
  - If it is real, why is it missing?
  - If it is imaginary, why do you think it should be part of your life?
- Are you deprived of anyone?
- If yes, who is it?
  - Is it a specific person, like a parent?
  - Or a type of person, like a soul mate?
- Are you deprived of a circumstance?
  - If yes, what kind? Personal? Professional?
- How does your sense of deprivation affect your eating?

Once you have identified the source of your deprivation, you need to consider how to deal with it.

What Can You Do When You Feel Deprived?

The solution to food deprivation is to revise your food plan. Remember, you are looking for a food plan you can live with for the rest of your life. You can contact a registered dietitian for advice. (www.eatright.org)

If you are not following a food plan, be sure to be kind to kind yourself and allow for moderate amounts of all food groups.

Also ask yourself why you are choosing to limit your food selections. It is possible your restriction of your food choices is a demonstration of some other issue. For example, perhaps you feel as if you have no control in your life so you exercise control over what you eat. Or you may be a perfectionist so you a need a "perfect" diet.

Identifying what lies beneath your food choices and addressing it directly is the same as identifying the underlying emotion and addressing it directly.

If you recognize any of this in yourself, good for you. That's excellent work. Now, find yourself a psychologist so you can address these issues. Doing so will take you a long way in this journey. By the way, the psychologist locator in the American Psychological Association's "Help Center" is a wonderful resource. (Visit www.apa.org.)

(*Note*: The exception to the idea that you should allow yourself to eat all foods in moderation is if you have any health issues, allergies, or medication considerations that require your diet to be modified. That is something to discuss with your physician.)

The key to not eating when you are feeling loss deprivation is to acknowledge that you are experiencing deprivation and then identify what it is (or who it is) that you are missing. Once you do that, you can take steps to deal with it.

Here's an example to illustrate what I mean. This time, let's take a look at a forty-five-year-old, single, childless woman who feels deprived of the pleasures of motherhood. If we take a step back, we can see that there are many ways she could bring a child into her life. For example, she could choose to have one on her own. She could adopt one. She could become a foster parent. She could join a Big Sisters organization or mentoring group. She could offer to babysit her neighbor's kids. Or she could volunteer at a neonatal unit. Is this the same as having her own child? Of course not, but these things are ways to address her sense of deprivation so she doesn't have to eat over it.

Here are some ways you can deal with loss deprivation:

1. *Go to therapy* – With the help of a psychologist, you can get to the root of your deprivation. Once you understand it, you can heal it.

2. *Brainstorm ways to get what you are missing* – Consider all your options—even if they seem outrageous. Try out some of your ideas and see what happens. You may be pleasantly surprised.

3. *Acceptance* – Work toward accepting the "nonexistence" of the person/situation you feel deprived of. Often we feel psychological pain because we are fighting reality. If you can embrace the truth of your situation, whatever it is, you will be in a better position to help yourself get through it.

4. *Forgiveness* – To forgive means to release a debt. In other words, when you forgive someone, you no longer punish them for their misdeeds. Do you forget? No. Do you make whatever happened okay? No. Instead, you release any attachment you have to the situation and move on. Practice forgiving the person who is missing or the circumstances that have not materialized. And forgive yourself for any role you may have played in your pain.

Let's move on to Linda. I hope you find her story inspiring.

* * * * *

Linda, a Case Study of Deprivation

After several months of therapy, Linda, a thirty-nine-year-old executive with a major motion picture company, broke down and cried for the entire session because her younger sister had just gotten engaged and Linda hadn't had a date in years. Linda was heartsick; she was certain her excessive weight was the reason she didn't have a husband and even more certain she would never have one.

What I knew about Linda's sister came from what Linda had shared in our sessions. Specifically, Linda talked a lot about her sister getting everything she ever wanted—from her high school prom date to admission to her first-choice college to her landing a great job straight out of school. Linda, on the other hand, had felt left behind her whole life. She talked frequently about being denied the things she wanted. For instance, she didn't go to her prom, she was waited-listed at her first choice of college, and she bounced around several movie studios before finding a job she liked. And all the while, Linda ate. She ate over each disappointment. She ate over each success her sister achieved. Linda was experiencing deprivation and making up for it with food.

As Linda's tears over her sister's engagement subsided, she was able to see the role deprivation had been playing in her struggles with food and dieting. Together we made a list of the things, people, and experiences Linda felt she was deprived of. Then we made another list of the things, people, and experiences she could invite into her life to give her life meaning, direction, and a sense of fullness.

Week by week, Linda moved through her list. As she did, she felt full without needing to overeat. Her sense of deprivation ended, and with it went a lot of excess weight. Linda may not be engaged like her younger sister, but her life feels richer, and she is definitely thinner.

* * * * *

Does anything about Linda's story seem familiar? Use the space below to clarify your own sense of deprivation. Is it food deprivation or loss deprivation or both? Be as specific as you can. Use your answers from above to help with this task.

About Me

_____

_____

_____

_____

_____

_____

_____

_____

_____

_____

_____

_____

_____

_____

_____

_____

Now that you have an idea of what *deprivation* is and the role it may play in your eating habits, it's time to make a plan for what you will do to deal with feeling deprived the next time you experience it. Use the space below to write down your ideas and remember to transfer your ideas to the "My Emotional Obstacles Action Plan" in the back of the book so they will be there when you need them.

Dealing with My Deprivation Action Plan

The strategies I can employ to deal with *deprivation* instead of eating are:

1.

2.

3.

4.

5.

CHAPTER SEVEN

Fear and Anxiety

A good deal of the work I do as a clinical psychologist has its roots in the work of Sigmund Freud. Freud taught us that much of what we think, feel, and do is affected by psychological forces that lie outside our awareness. He referred to this as our unconscious. According to Freud, our unconscious mind shapes our personality, and until these unconscious influences are recognized (in other words "made conscious") and healed, they will continue to run the show. The place where I see the unconscious working overtime is in the matter of fear and anxiety. Many people walk around feeling frightened and worried and they don't really know why. My job is to help them understand the "why."

In this chapter, we will explore fear and anxiety and the role they play in your eating habits. But don't worry; I won't psychoanalyze you. Instead, I will just help you recognize these emotions and show you what you can do about them.

What Is Fear?

Boo. Did I scare you? I hope not. But if I did, what you experienced was fear. To feel fear is to feel frightened. Fear can be a physical "alarm" or warning of danger. You can be frightened of a lot of things—spiders, dogs, thunder, lightning, or the dark. Some people can be frightened of commitment, rejection, or public speaking. In psychological circles, we call those fears phobias.

When you have a fear or a phobia, it is of a specific situation or event; so you are aware of the threat because it is right in front of you. It is happening now. The electric power goes out and you are in the dark; you feel afraid. You see a spider crawling up the wall; you feel scared. A stray dog is walking toward you; you are frightened. Or you are going to a party, and you are afraid to talk to people—that is called social phobia.

Some people confuse fear with anxiety. But as you will see, anxiety is a very particular kind of fear.

What Is Anxiety?

Anxiety is specifically fear of the future. The Merriam-Webster Dictionary (www.m-w.com) defines anxiety as, "an uneasy state of mind usually over the possibility of an *anticipated* misfortune or trouble" (emphasis added).

The key word is *anticipated*. When you are afraid of something that you expect to happen in the future, you are anxious. In other words, it is the apprehension of unpleasant or dangerous events that you *anticipate happening sometime later.*

Typically, anxiety is created by the thoughts that you tell yourself in response to a particular situation or occurrence. It is a way of explaining things to yourself that scares you. For example, you have to give a presentation at work next week, and all week long, you imagine the worst. You "see" yourself forgetting your speaking points. You think about all the things that could go wrong such as getting stuck in traffic, having the computer fail, or being asked a question you do not have an answer for. Before you know it, you have worked yourself into such a tizzy you can't sleep, and you're moody and irritable. Yeesh. How awful. The bad news is you did this to yourself. The good news is you did this to yourself, which means you can undo it. More on that later.

What Do Your Fear and Anxiety Look Like?

We all feel fear from time to time, and to tell you the truth, fear is a good thing. Fear alerts us to hazards that need our attention. Think about it. If you are driving and a car swerves in front of you and you feel fear, that's a good thing because you will take action to avoid an accident.

Typically, in an incident like this one, you will feel temporarily frightened. What is happening is that your sympathetic nervous system is being turned on. The sympathetic nervous system is commonly known as our "fight-or-flight" response. It's that part of our body that activates all the systems that we need in order to deal with an emergency. Our heart rate goes up. Our pupils dilate. And our digestion slows down. Once the emergency is over, the parasympathetic nervous system kicks in, and our body is restored to normal. This is your body's way of dealing with a real threat.

It is when our fears go beyond the real threats that we face and take over our day-to-day lives that we have a problem. And it's usually in these instances that food becomes a way to cope.

Sometimes a frightening experience can take over a person's life. Daniel's was one such case. One afternoon, Daniel was driving along the Pacific Coast Highway when a car pulled out of a parking lot into his path. The two cars collided. Neither driver was injured, but Daniel's car was totaled. Even though he wasn't hurt physically, Daniel suffered psychological injuries. In particular, he had nightmares and developed a phobia of getting into a car. It got so bad that Daniel couldn't leave his house. He spent most of his time on his couch eating. To help him heal, Daniel and I initially did phone sessions. Eventually, he was able to drive to my office and, ultimately, resume his life. When he did that, he stopped eating because of fear.

Unlike fear, which is typically a response to something in a person's environment, anxiety is worry about the future. And while its cause is, in a way, "all in your head," you definitely can feel it in your body. The physical symptoms of anxiety—sweaty palms, dizziness, headaches, heart palpitations, and light-headedness—are quite real, but they start with your thoughts.

The American Psychological Association's definition of anxiety includes its physical manifestations. "[Anxiety is] characterized by feelings of tension, worried thoughts and physical changes. Anxiety disorders such as panic disorder and obsessive compulsive disorder (OCD) cause recurring intrusive thoughts or concerns and physical symptoms such as sweating, trembling, dizziness or a rapid heartbeat."

So, in addition to intrusive thoughts about some future event, an anxious person will feel physical symptoms such as sweating, trembling, dizziness, or a rapid heartbeat. When the anxious person eats to calm down, the cycle of eating in response to anxiety begins.

Think about your own life. What are the situations and circumstances that leave you feeling afraid or worried? Do those feelings affect how you eat? Do you eat to calm yourself down? If you do, read on for ideas on what else you can do instead.

What Can Do When You Feel Fear or Anxiety?

As you have seen, the truth is, you create your own anxiety by the way you talk to yourself. This is actually very good news because, if you can talk yourself into anxiety, you can talk yourself out of it. For example, let's say you are going on a job interview and you are understandably nervous. But as you are driving to the interview you start getting really nervous. Why? What's going on that has you getting more afraid? Is it more likely something else you are thinking about as you drive to the interview? Your conversation with yourself might go something like this:

> *I gotta get this job. If I don't get this job, I don't know what I'll do. I only have a little bit of money left in my savings account. What will I do if I don't get this job? How will I pay the rent? Where will I live if I can't afford my apartment anymore? Where will I go? I'll end up on the street. How will I survive? What will I do?*
>
> *There's a doughnut shop. I want one now. I need one if I'm going to survive this day.*

By now, you are a wreck and on your way to a binge. You've gone from simple, normal nervousness over a job interview to being homeless and living on the streets. Sound absurd? Well, unfortunately this kind of self-talk is quite common.

What would a more healthful, supportive inner dialogue sound like? How about something like this:

> *Boy am I nervous. I really want this job. I know I have the qualifications, but the competition*

is stiff. I really hope I get this job. But if I don't, I know I'll be okay. I still have some money left in my savings account, so I won't be on the streets. I will continue to look for work. I'll send out more résumés. Oh. I know; I'll call Susan. She'll have some good ideas for my job search. In the meanwhile, I'll give this interview my best shot and go from there.

This second conversation is much more supportive and constructive. It builds you up and gives you hope rather than tearing you down and making you want to binge. It is this kind of positive self-talk that alleviates anxiety, builds self-esteem, and reduces the urge to binge. (If you'd like to learn more about building your self-esteem, you might enjoy my book *Self-Fullness: The Art of Loving and Caring for Your "Self."* Written like a workbook, *Self-Fullness* teaches you how to get to know yourself better and put yourself first.)

Before we move on to the self-help techniques you can use to address your fears and anxieties, I'd like to mention the importance of getting professional help—psychological and medical—if your fears and anxieties are severe. If your emotions get in the way of you living your life, like Daniel's did for him, it is very important that you consider working with a mental health professional. In addition to receiving psychotherapy, you may be referred to a psychiatrist for a medication evaluation. Antianxiety medications are an excellent adjunct to psychotherapy for many people who struggle with anxiety disorders. To know for sure if that's you, see your physician for a referral.

If your fears and/or anxieties are more like nuisances than life-threatening circumstances, the following self-help strategies can do wonders.

Thought Stopping 101

The first approach to dealing with anxiety is to treat your thoughts—to change how you explain things to yourself so that you see things in a more positive, reassuring way. For example, say things to yourself such as, "Everything will be okay," or, "All I am experiencing is anxiety; it can't hurt me."

This technique is called thought stopping and is based on cognitive therapy. Thought stopping takes practice, but once you master it, you will definitely enjoy its benefits. You will find that, when you get used to talking to yourself in this affirming way, much of your anxiety will disappear.

Here's how it works:

1. Identify a thought that is making you anxious or frightened.
2. Say, "Stop," either silently to yourself or aloud (if you are alone).
3. Replace the anxiety-provoking thought with a different, more encouraging thought.
4. Hold the new thought in your mind for as long as you can.
5. Repeat each time you catch an anxious thought popping into your head.

Now you try.

1. Identify a thought that is making you anxious or frightened. Write it here: _____
   _____
   _____
2. Say, "Stop," either silently to yourself or aloud (if you are alone).

3. Think of a different, more encouraging thought. Write that thought here: _____

_____

_____

4. Hold the new thought in your mind for a count of ten.

5. Repeat the new thought each time you catch the original anxious thought popping into your head.

More Anxiety-Reducing Tools

Learning to Relax

Another approach to dealing with anxiety is to learn to relax by practicing a relaxation technique. One to try is a Systematic Muscle Relaxing Journey. You can find many different CDs and DVDs that use this technique. In the resource section of this book, I list some to get you started. Try one. Use it regularly to teach yourself how to relax. If you don't want to buy a CD or DVD, you can make your own.

In a gentle, calm, and reassuring voice, read the following into a recorder:

> Close your eyes. Lie back on a sofa or floor and just relax. Pay attention to your breathing. Listen to your breaths as they float in and out, in and out. Allow the thoughts from the day to pass gently through your mind. In and out. Count to yourself, slowly, from one to ten, relaxing deeply with each count. Ready?
>
> One, two, three, four, five, six, seven, eight, nine, ten.

Now starting with your feet, relax each part of your body. Begin by tightly clenching your toes for a count of ten (one, two, three, four, five, six, seven, eight, nine, ten). Now release. Feel the tingling as your feet let go of the tensions of the day.

Let's repeat your feet. Again, clench your toes for a count of ten (one, two, three, four, five, six, seven, eight, nine, ten). Now release. Doesn't that feel good?

Now move up to your calves. Tighten your calves for the count of ten and then release. Ready? Tighten (one, two, three, four, five, six, seven, eight, nine, ten.) Release. Feel the relaxation move up your body from your feet through your calves. Let's repeat your calves. Ready? Tighten (one, two, three, four, five, six, seven, eight, nine, ten.) Release.

Allow the relaxation to fill up your body. Breathe deeply. In and out. In and out. Feel yourself get more and more relaxed with each breath.

Allow yourself to relax a bit more and then continue with your thighs. Tighten your thighs for a count of ten (one, two, three, four, five, six, seven, eight, nine, ten). Release.

Allow the relaxation to move farther up your body. Enjoy the tingling. Enjoy the breathing. If a thought pops into your mind, gently push it out. There will be plenty of time to think about it later, after your relaxation is complete. For now, just relax and truly enjoy this time you are giving yourself.

When you are ready, move on to your arms. Clench your fists and tighten your arms as hard as you can. Hold for a count of ten (one, two, three, four, five, six, seven, eight, nine, ten) and release. Let the relaxation float up your arms.

Continue to relax your legs. You should be feeling pretty good by now. Continue to breathe. In and out. In and out.

Now relax your shoulders. As hard as you can, squeeze your shoulder blades together for a count of ten (one, two, three, four, five, six, seven, eight, nine, ten). Release. Shrug them up and down a few times to get more kinks out. Release.

Feel yourself sink further and further into the surface on which you are lying. Relax. Just relax.

Next, scrunch your face as hard as you can. Don't worry. No one is watching. You are alone relaxing. Scrunch for a count of ten (one, two, three, four, five, six, seven, eight, nine, ten). Release. Can you feel the tension leaving your face?

Let's do your face again. Ready? Scrunch for ten (one, two, three, four, five, six, seven. eight, nine, ten.) Release. Relax. Relax deeply and serenely.

Allow yourself to enjoy the floating sensation that is welling inside of you. Enjoy the quiet. Enjoy the tranquility. If there is any part of your body that is still feeling tense, isolate it and then tighten and release. Tighten and release.

Now continue to relax. Let the thoughts float in and out of your mind. Let the peacefulness take over and just relax. Lie here for a few minutes and enjoy the rest.

When you are ready, count gently from ten down to one and open your eyes (ten, nine, eight, seven, six, five, four, three, two, one). Open your eyes. You feel relaxed and ready to take on life. Go for it.

Once you are finished, lie down in a darkened room, play back the recording, and enjoy yourself as you relax.

In addition to using the relaxation exercise that you just learned, there are four other ways for you to reduce the anxiety in your life. They are:

- *Physical activity* – Running, walking, swimming, and gardening are all helpful in reducing anxiety because they expend energy. Anxiety can be thought of as an energy buzzing through you. If you expend some of that energy through physical exercise, less will "buzz," and you will feel better.

- *Eliminate caffeine* – For many people, the side effects of caffeine mimic anxiety. These side effects include a racing heart, sweaty palms, a nervous stomach, and sleepless nights. If you suffer from any of these conditions, you may want to eliminate caffeine from your life and see if you feel calmer. Check labels.

There is caffeine in some items you might never think about, such as headache medicine and tea.

- *Practice yoga* – For centuries, people have used the practice of yoga to help calm themselves down and restore peace to their wayward minds. Today, yoga studios are as ubiquitous as Starbucks. A few minutes of yoga each day can have a wonderfully cumulative effect on your haggard nerves. You can attend a class (many studios offer a free initial class or an affordable monthly pass) or you can practice on your own at home. You can find yoga instruction on your television and online. There are hundreds of DVDs you can purchase. I have listed some of them in the resource section.

- *Meditate* – Mediation is a practice of quieting your mind. It is not necessarily a silencing of your mind. It is more like a softening and slowing down of your anxious thoughts that are run amuck. A few minutes of sitting silently can reduce your anxious thoughts and alleviate your fears. If you find it too hard to just sit, use a guided meditation to help you. Focusing on the narrator's voice is a way to channel your attention away from your anxiety. You can find such mediation on iTunes and Amazon.com and in many bookstores and libraries. I listed a few for you in the resource section.

To get a better idea of how to cope with anxiety, let's meet Kim. She was highly anxious when she started treatment. Let's see how she did.

* * * * *

Kim, a Case Study of Anxiety

One of my most endearing patients was Kim. At the time I was working with her, she was in her late forties, single, and highly anxious. Everything worried her. Kim's sessions were filled week after week with concerns about her cats, her house, her aging parents, and her job. Did Kim have things to worry about? Sure; we all do. But Kim took it to an extreme. She was in a constant state of anxiety, suffering from panic attacks, insomnia, and compulsive overeating. She was five foot four, and her weight topped 250 pounds.

The first thing I did was refer Kim to a psychiatrist for medication to help reduce some of her anxiety symptoms. I did this because her symptoms were so severe that she was unable to concentrate on the therapy. Over time, the medication helped reduce her panic attacks, and she was able to get some sleep. Once that happened, we could get to work on healing the underlying causes of her anxiety.

Then I had Kim keep a thought diary. She was to write down all of her thoughts over the course of a week so that she could begin to see how her thoughts were feeding her anxiety. It only took her three days to get the message. She saw that her mind was a "doomsday machine." Every thought she had was negative or troublesome. To reduce her anxiety, she practiced thought stopping and relaxation techniques. Each time, she had an anxiety-producing thought she would catch herself; acknowledge it; and replace it with a different, more calming thought. In addition, every day she did a ten-minute relaxation session similar to the one above.

Slowly and surely she calmed down. She started to see her life more clearly and recognized the difference between a real threat to her well-being and a thought-manufactured one. As she calmed down, so did her eating. Soon she joined a national weight-loss program and was on her way to her ideal weight.

* * * * *

How about you? Can you relate? What fears and anxieties plague you? Write down the ones that are causing you the most distress so you can start to work on them right away.

About Me

_____

_____

_____

_____

_____

_____

_____

_____

_____

_____

_____

_____

_____

_____

_____

Now that you have an idea of what _fear_ and _anxiety_ are and the role they may play in your eating habits, it's time to make a plan for what you will do when you feel afraid or worried.

Use the space below to write down your ideas and include them in your "My Emotional Obstacles Action Plan." Refer to that action plan whenever you need some help.

Dealing with My Fear Action Plan

The strategies I can employ to deal with *fear* instead of eating are:

1.

2.

3.

4.

5.

Dealing with My Anxiety Action Plan

The strategies I can employ to deal with *anxiety* instead of eating are:

1.

2.

3.

4.

5.

CHAPTER EIGHT

Hopelessness

I'd like to check in with you again. How are things going? You have wrestled with the first four emotional obstacles. And we are about to dive into the fifth. I want to make sure you are still with me. If at any time you feel this material is bringing up feelings that you would like help with, please reach out. Take this book to a psychologist. For referrals you can go to the American Psychological Association's website (www.apa.org) or your state or local association. Professional assistance can be very valuable as you tackle your emotional life. Professional guidance can give you hope.

Speaking of hope, the next emotion we are undertaking is hopelessness. So often in my work with emotional overeaters, I hear sighs of resignation. Inside those sighs I know are thoughts such as, *Life will never get better, things will never work out, and the weight will never come off.* I also know from dedicating my professional life to helping people overcome psychological issues that there is always hope. Let me help you find yours if right now you feel as if don't have any.

What Is Hopelessness?

Hopelessness means having no expectation of success, as if there is no solution to what plagues you. You may experience hopelessness in many settings. For example, you may have projects to accomplish at work and very little time to complete them, and so you feel hopeless. Or you have been on hundreds of dates and haven't found "the one," and so you feel as if he or she does not exist. That's hopelessness. If you have ever found yourself at the bottom of an empty bag of chips staring into its greasy, salty abyss and wondering what's left for you if there are no more chips, you may relate to the feeling of hopelessness.

Hopelessness that isn't addressed can lead to despair. Despair if not dealt with can lead to serious consequences, such as major depression and, in the worst cases, suicide. Recognizing hopelessness and relieving its effect by finding hope is critical as you learn to eliminate the emotional obstacles to your weight-loss goals.

An important note: If your sense of hopelessness ever gets to the point where you see no reason to go on and are considering suicide, please run don't walk to your nearest emergency room and let someone help you. There is always hope, but sometimes you need someone else to point it out to you.

How Does Hopelessness Feel?

The people I have worked with who have described feeling hopeless to me typically describe a hollow feeling deep inside their gut. They say it leaves them feeling shaky and vulnerable. And their body language reflects that. They tend to sit with sunken shoulders and downcast eyes. Their arms are often folded around them, as if to give themselves a much-needed hug.

Others say they feel agitated when they are hopeless. One person, Elliot, told me he feels like a caged animal pacing back and forth with nowhere to go.

What Does Your Hopelessness Look Like?

In understanding what hopeless may look like for you, consider these questions:

- Does either of the above descriptions fit for you or is your experience something else?
- When do you experience hopelessness?
- Does hopelessness crop up frequently for you?
- Is it a knee-jerk reaction to feeling overwhelmed by something?
- Or is it a rare occurrence that happens only when you have tried everything and are at your wit's end?

Take some time to think about your answer. You may discover that the moments when you feel hopeless vary. And how your hopelessness feels to you may vary as well. That happens. The key is that you are recognizing this emotion and you can now choose to address it.

If you feel hopeless a lot, pay attention to the thoughts you are telling yourself. Some people give up too quickly and sink into a hopeless state of mind. Just because something doesn't work out the first time you try it (or even the tenth time) doesn't mean the situation is hopeless. I have a friend who took the bar exam twenty-five times before he passed it. He never gave up hope, and now he has a successful law practice and a life he is proud of. Just like with anxiety, the thoughts we tell ourselves when we are faced with difficult circumstances can make the difference between a healthy, positive response to the situation or a nosedive straight into a binge.

What Can You Do When You Feel Hopeless?

To understand hopelessness and what to do about it, we need to take a really close look at what is causing this feeling within you. Is the situation really as dire as you predict? Sometimes we get so caught up in our pain that we cannot see the situation as it really is. Sometimes we are only a moment away from relief but don't even know it. The key to removing hopelessness as an obstacle to your weight-loss efforts is to find hope. Any hope. Anywhere.

Lets' consider these questions again.

- When do you experience hopelessness?
- Does hopelessness crop up frequently?
- Is it a knee-jerk reaction to feeling overwhelmed?
- Is it a rare occurrence that happens only when you have tried everything and are at your wit's end?
- Is the situation really as dire as you think it is?
- Are you so caught up in your distress that you cannot see the condition as it really is?
- Are you only a moment away from relief but don't know it?

If you answered yes to the last three questions, it may be time to bring in some help. There is an expression that sometimes we "can't see the forest for the trees." This expression means that we are so caught up in what is right in front of us that we cannot see the bigger picture. When that happens, another person's perspective can be very valuable. Run your predicament by a trusted friend or confidant. See if he or she can offer you another way of looking at your problem. Sometimes that may be all you need to find hope.

Let's take a closer look at the concept of hope. To find hope means to have the feeling that something desirable *could* happen, that there is *some chance* of things getting better—even if that chance feels very remote. Hope suggests *possibility*. As you think about your own experience with hopelessness, can you find a glimmer of hope? Is there any light at the end of the tunnel? Is there even a tunnel?

You can find hope in many places, some of which may seem unlikely. Here are examples of places in which some of my patients were able to find hope:

- church
- synagogue
- the pages of a book
- the lyrics of a song
- the words of a poet
- the scenes of a movie
- the comments of a friend
- the laughter of a child
- the lick from a puppy
- a purr of a kitten
- their journal
- praying to God or their Higher Power
- finishing a 5K
- signing up for a 5K
- doing volunteer work
- being diagnosed with an illness
- giving money to a homeless vet
- registering for a class

- a cup of tea
- the birth of a grandchild
- a twelve-step meeting
- a group therapy session
- the story of another's triumph over adversity
- the smile of a stranger
- a hug from a friend

Add your ideas of where you might find hope here:

-

-

-

-

-

To find hope means to find the possibility of a better future.

Meet MJ, a classic case of hopelessness.

* * * * *

Mary Jean, a Case Study of Hopelessness

Mary Jean—or MJ, as her friends like to call her—was a classic case of hopelessness. MJ, like so many others I have worked with, felt hopeless about her weight. At fifty-six years old and five foot seven, MJ carried about forty extra pounds on her frame. You couldn't really see it, but she sure felt it.

From the time MJ was fourteen, she'd dieted. Her weight would fluctuate about twenty pounds—until she hit menopause. And then it shot up another twenty. MJ was at her wit's end. She felt as if she was destined to be overweight for the rest of her life.

She was on the verge of quitting therapy and giving up on the idea of ever being slim when I asked her a question. "MJ, if your beloved niece were failing algebra, would you give up on her?" I wanted to know. "Would you stop helping her find a way to understand the subject? Would you tell her it is hopeless and she should quit school?"

MJ smiled. She knew where I was going with this. "No, of course not," she told me.

"So, what would you do?" I asked further.

She replied, "I'd get her a tutor."

"Okay. Well, what if you got yourself a tutor too?"

MJ pondered my suggestion for a moment and said, "A personal trainer is like a tutor, isn't she?"

She then "remembered" that the gym she'd joined earlier in the year (but rarely went to) had offered her a free session with a personal trainer as a bonus for joining. MJ decided to take advantage of that offer. She went to the training session still filled with a sense of hopelessness and thinking to herself that she'd tried exercising before and it hadn't worked.

But this time, something was different. This time, her personal trainer was a slightly older woman who completely understood what happens to a woman's body during menopause. She introduced MJ to the idea of interval training, where you do short bursts (thirty to sixty seconds) of intense activity in between longer periods of moderate to easy exercise. MJ was intrigued; this she could. The free session was a huge success. MJ felt excited and motivated to do intervals on her own.

When she came in for her next session with me, she was giddy. She told me about her success at the gym and how she had found something that would help her with her weight-loss goals. What she'd found was hope.

* * * * *

Does MJ's story give you any hope? What could improve your future? What could give you hope? Where might you find it? Write your thoughts here.

About Me

_____

_____

_____

_____

_____

_____

_____

_____

_____

_____

_____

_____

_____

_____

_____

_____

_____

_____

_____

_____

_____

_____

_____

_____

_____

_____

_____

_____

_____

_____

Now that you have an idea of what *hopelessness* is and the role it may play in your eating habits, it's time to make a plan for what you will do when you lose hope. Use the space below to write down your ideas, and then, like before, transfer your ideas to the "My Emotional Obstacles Action Plan" in the back of the book. Having all your strategies in one place will make things easier for you when you are having a hard time.

Dealing with My Hopelessness Action Plan

The strategies I can employ to deal with *hopelessness* instead of eating are:

1.

2.

3.

4.

5.

CHAPTER NINE

Loneliness

Welcome to the next emotional obstacle we will explore—loneliness. In the introduction to the last chapter, I mentioned reaching out to a psychologist for help with your journey. As we embark on our exploration of loneliness, I'd like to mention the idea of group therapy as a tool for self-discovery.

Group therapy is a form of psychotherapy where typically six to eight people meet once a week for an hour and a half with a specially trained psychologist to work out their "issues" together. I love group therapy so much that I got a postdoctoral certification in group and have been running groups for over twenty years. You can find groups for all sorts of topics—personal growth, self-esteem, eating disorders, to name a few.

A great resource for finding a group therapist is through the National Registry of Group Psychotherapists. Go to the website for the American Group Psychotherapy Association (www.agpa.org) and click on the "find a certified group psychotherapist" link. You'll enter your zip code and the type of group you are interested in, and groups in your area will be listed.

What Is Loneliness?

The dreaded "L" word. Loneliness is a powerful emotion and can strike when we are alone or even when we are in the company of others. It occurs typically as distress caused by the absence of interpersonal relationships. Eating because you are lonely is more common than you might think. Since so much emotional overeating is done when a person is alone, we have here a truly vicious cycle.

How Does Loneliness Feel?

I used the word *dread* to describe loneliness when I introduced the topic above. The reason I used this word is that it is the word I hear most often when a patient is describing time alone. People tell me how they *dread* the weekends because they have no one to spend time with or they *dread* when they have to use their accrued vacation from work because they have no one to go away with. They go on to describe the pain they feel and the binge they have planned to deal with the pain.

I also hear people talk about being lonely when they are in a relationship. Perhaps their spouses work long hours and come home tired and not eager to engage in conversation. Others complain about the lack of intimacy in their relationships and feelings of being trapped in a loveless marriage or roommate-like arrangement. In each situation, the pain is caused by a lack of meaningful connections with others. It hurts to be alone. It hurts to be in a relationship that isn't meeting your emotional needs. In the moment, a big bowl of ice cream topped with crumbled cookies and whipped cream sounds good.

But, in the long run, eating to cope with loneliness is not the answer. Inviting good people into your life is the better way to go. I call it "increasing the flow of people into your life."

What Does Your Loneliness Look Like?

If loneliness is a trigger for your overeating, when does it happen?

- Do you spend weekend after weekend home alone?
- Or are weekday evenings tougher for you?
- If you are in a relationship, is the relationship satisfying, or is something missing?

Think about with whom you spend most of your time.

- Are these people friends or acquaintances?
- Coworkers or clients? Neighbors or Facebook requests?

Think about what you want from these people, keeping in mind that people come into our lives at different times and for different reasons. Having a BFF may have worked in high school, but as an adult, it is unlikely that you will have such a friend. Or maybe your best friend is a cat. One young woman told me how happy she'd been since she'd adopted a stray cat. She said the cat keeps her company at night so she doesn't feel so alone. I am a huge animal lover and was thrilled she brought a cat into her life, but what I really wanted for her was human contact. I want that for you too.

What Can You Do When You Feel Lonely?

There are a variety of ways to cope if loneliness is the reason you overeat. If your loneliness is caused by a lack of great people in your life, then the commonsense response is to invite more people into your life and end your isolation. What can you do to "increase the flow of people into your life"?

Here are some suggestions to get you started:

- Join a church or synagogue and attend regularly.
- Take a class.
- Volunteer for a cause you believe in.
- Get a dog, and go to the dog park on Saturday afternoons.
- Offer to babysit a neighbor's children.
- Spend time with your family.
- Contact old friends you haven't heard from in a while.
- Join a psychotherapy group to build relationship skills.

Add your own ideas here:

-

-

-

-

If the reason you feel lonely is that you want to be in a romantic relationship and are not, here are a few things to consider.

1. *What are you doing to find your romantic partner?*
    I work with a lot of women who say they want a relationship but then don't go about getting one. I joke and say that, unless their dream date is with the UPS guy, they better leave the house. Men are the same. They tell me they are looking for "Ms. Right." But when I ask what they are doing to find her, they offer all kinds of excuses—from being too busy at work to hating Internet dating. To find your partner, you need to put in the same effort as if you were looking for a job. Sure that's not romantic, but you have to kiss a lot of frogs to find your prince or princess. So start kissing …

2. *Do you really want a romantic partner?*
    Sure you say you do, but do you really? Some people are actually happier alone. They prefer to do things their way and are not very comfortable sharing. That's okay. Just own it.

3. *Are you too picky?*
    I'd like to offer you a difficult truth—sometimes we are not in relationships because we are looking for that perfect person and, well, a perfect person does not exist. Really think about who you are looking for. Think in terms of character and values rather than status and looks. I believe that, once you shift your criteria, your luck will change.

On the other hand, if your loneliness is because of the relationship you are in, here are a few things for you to think about.

1. *Are you looking to get all your emotional needs from your partner?*

   This is a common mistake. I see it all the time. Women look to their husbands and boyfriends to meet all their emotional needs. And as a general statement, most men are just not up for the job. Men tend to be fixers, and most of the time we women just want to be heard. Here's a tip: Figure out what your partner is good at (for example, problem-solving, helping around the house, running errands, disciplining the kids) and go to him for these things, and then invite other people (sisters, girlfriends, therapists, clergy) in to meet your other needs.

   Men make a similar mistake. They expect their wives and girlfriends to share all their interests. If he is a football fan, he wants her to be one too. If he likes action flicks, so should she. To feel closer to your partner, stop looking for her to be a mirror image of you. Find buddies with whom you can watch football and see action flicks. Then find other activities that interest you both. Try something new together. You may be pleasantly surprised.

2. *Are you expecting your partner to know what you need and want and are disappointed because those needs and wants are not being met?*

   Here's another common problem I see. I call this one "mind reading." I hear it all the time. "He should know …" (You can fill in the blank.) No, actually he "shouldn't." This goes the other way too. "She should know …" Again, no she shouldn't. Expecting your partner to know what you need or want is asking your partner to read your mind. State your needs. If they go ignored after you have expressed them, well, that's another issue. But, if your partner doesn't know don't punish him or her for failing to give you what you want.

3. *What efforts have you made to reconnect with your partner in an emotional way?*
    Relationships, especially long-lasting ones, take work. It's easy to fall into a rut with a partner you've known for years. Instead, put some effort in. Plan a date night. Take an interest in your partner's life. Join him or her for a hobby or a favorite sport. And, remember why you fell in love in the first place. Think about all the things that made you feel, *He's the one* or, *She's the woman of my dreams.* Most likely, those reasons are still there. Dust them off. You'll both be happy you did.

It's time to take a look at Patty. Does her situation seem familiar?

* * * * *

Patty, a Case Study of Loneliness

Patty is a dear, sweet woman. If you met her, you would like her immediately. The problem for Patty is that she is always alone. She works as a medical notes transcriber from her home. Her home is at the end of a narrow street with only a few other homes on it. Patty's world is very small, and she feels isolated. She spends her days on her computer writing the notes and then sends them via fax or e-mail to the recipient. Most days, she doesn't see a soul. Even the mailman doesn't come over because her mailbox is curbside.

To fill the loneliness, Patty eats. And as a result, she has over a hundred pounds of excess weight. Being overweight doesn't help the matter because she is reluctant to go out and have anyone see her as she is.

It may be obvious to you that what Patty needs are some friends. It was obvious to Patty too, but she wasn't sure how to make friends, where to find them, and whether they would want to be her friends when they saw how heavy she was. Patty and I began very slowly.

We started our work by having Patty make some online friends. Using a chat room she discovered that people liked her. Then she ventured into some structured activities, first at her church and then at a local community center. Finally she got a laptop and moved her work out of her of house and into a local coffee shop. There, she engaged in conversation and became a regular.

As people got to know her, she created a circle of friends who she sees regularly. She doesn't eat as much as she used to because she is "full" now with people rather than food.

* * * * *

Is there anything about Patty's story that could help you? If you eat because you are lonely, did this chapter give you any ideas on how to overcome that obstacle to your weight-loss goals? Are you interested in giving group therapy a try? Put your thoughts here.

About Me

_____
_____
_____
_____
_____
_____
_____
_____
_____
_____
_____
_____
_____
_____
_____
_____
_____
_____
_____
_____
_____
_____
_____
_____
_____
_____
_____
_____
_____

Now that you have an idea of what *loneliness* is and the role it may play in your eating habits, it's time to make a plan for what you will do the next time you feel lonely. Use the space below to write down your strategies and then record them in your "My Emotional Obstacles Action Plan." Your action plan can be a lifeline during lonely times.

Dealing with My Loneliness Action Plan

The strategies I can employ to deal with *loneliness* instead of eating are:

1.

2.

3.

4.

5.

CHAPTER TEN

Sadness and Depression

We all feel sad from time to time—whether it's because we suffered some kind of loss or disappointment or just finished watching a touching movie. For some of us, sadness is momentary. For others, sadness prevails. It becomes a way of life. When that happens, we have to be mindful that our sadness is not turning into depression.

What Is Sadness?

Sadness is a normal part of life. It can be a response to a setback or failure. Endings can trigger sadness, as can regret. Synonyms for sadness include unhappiness, melancholy, and sorrow.

Most of the time, sadness is fleeting. Within minutes, our mood can change if something interrupts our sadness such as a smile, a humorous friend, or a funny scene in a sitcom. At times, our sadness may linger, especially when the trigger is a significant event such as a death or the end of something.

How Does Sadness Feel?

Sadness is a difficult emotion to describe. I hear a lot of different versions. Some people describe their sadness as an ache in their gut. They talk about hollowness inside their stomach. They also tell me that the hollowness goes away when they eat. Others speak of tension in their throats. They say they have a hard time speaking or their voices are crackly or hoarse. For some, it shows up as teary eyes and/or weepiness. Some sob. Others choke back tears.

What Does Your Sadness Look Like?

Besides the physical expressions of sadness mentioned above, have you ever thought about what your sadness looks like? For instance, are certain thoughts consistently present when you are sad? Something to think about is which comes first—the thought or the sadness.

Or, are there certain behaviors or rituals you engage in when you are feeling sad? I had one patient who, when sad, would hole up in her apartment, draw the drapes, and read romance novels all weekend long.

Another patient would cancel all his appointments and go surfing (I'm in Southern California remember). When he would cancel one of our sessions to surf, I knew right away what we would be talking about the next time I saw him.

What about you? There are no right or wrong answers, only your answers. Remember, the reason we investigate what your emotions feel and look like is so (1) you can recognize them when they happen and (2) you can allow yourself to feel them when they show up.

Before we move onto what you can do when you are sad, I'd like to address an important related topic—depression.

What Is Depression?

In the introduction to this chapter, I said that, when sadness becomes a way of life, we must be on alert for the presence of depression. Depression, unlike sadness, is a serious psychological condition that necessitates psychological and sometimes medical intervention.

How Does Depression Feel?

So what is the difference between sadness and depression? You can think of it this way: Sadness is like a rainy day. You feel a bit blue, maybe down in the dumps for a while, and then move out of it as the "clouds" that caused it move on. Depression is a like a rainy season. It goes on and on with little or no relief and feels like it will last forever.

What Does Depression Look Like?

Depression comes in several forms. First, it can show up as a general malaise, where you are just not yourself for a very long time. Sometimes this is referred to as dysthymic depression.

Or it can come in the form of irritation and agitation, such that you find yourself short-tempered with everyone and everything around you. Psychologists may refer to this as atypical depression.

Sometimes, it can be more serious. In these cases, you find yourself unable to accomplish even the most basic things in your life, such as getting up to go to work or showering before getting dressed in the morning. You may feel tired, in pain, or sensitive. You may experience changes in your sleeping and eating patterns as well. Your concentration disappears, as does interest in things you used to enjoy. This may be a clinical form of depression, known as major depressive disorder, which has very specific symptoms. These symptoms, which last for at least two weeks, include:

1. Feelings of sadness, emptiness, tearfulness, or weepiness
2. A loss of interest in activities you used to find pleasurable
3. A significant change in your appetite, leading to an increase or decrease in your weight
4. Insomnia
5. Feelings of restlessness, fatigue, or loss of energy
6. Feelings of worthlessness or guilt
7. Diminished ability to think or concentrate
8. Indecisiveness
9. Recurrent thoughts of death or suicide

If you recognize yourself as having any of these symptoms, or if your depression is so severe it is significantly impacting your life, I urge you to get professional help. A good psychologist and some medication could do wonders for a severe depression. See your physician for a referral or call your local chapter of the American Psychological Association for assistance. The APA's website is also an excellent resource for information in general about depression and many of the other topics I am discussing with you. Check it out.

Please keep in mind that food, no matter how much you eat, will not "cure" depression. Food won't "cure" sadness either. Sorry. But there *are* things you can do to help yourself feel better, and we will address those soon. For now, let's continue to look further into what sadness is.

What Can You Do When You Feel Sadness or Depression?

Fortunately, for sadness and the less serious forms of depression, there is quite a bit you can do to help yourself cope. Let me show you how:

1. The first step is to identify your feelings. This is where recognizing how your sadness or depression feels comes in handy. Specifically, which one is it and how severe is it?
   a. If you are sad or only slightly depressed (like the malaise described above), read on.
   b. If your depression is more serious than a malaise, do not attempt to use self-help to get through it. Find a psychologist and a medical doctor to assist you.
2. Next, consider why you are feeling sad or mildly depressed. Have you suffered a loss lately? Did someone criticize you and you are feeling badly now? Are you disappointed about something?
3. Once you have identified the source of your feelings, describe it. Write about, talk about, or draw about it. Any expression of it is helpful.
4. Now feel the feelings. Talk about them. Cry about them. Shout about them. Do whatever allows you to experience them.
5. Then, when you are ready for the feelings to pass, take action. Action is an effective antidote for sadness and mild depression. Do something. Go for a walk. Make a phone call. Dance in your living room. Paint a picture. Anything. Just get moving.

Take a look at how Robyn coped with her sadness and overcame a primary reason she overate. Then, in contrast, read about Jessie, whose depression required medication and intensive psychotherapy.

* * * * *

Robyn, a Case Study of Sadness

In my office are several boxes of tissues—three to be exact. They are strategically located so that, wherever a patient sits, a tissue is only an arm's length away. For Robyn, that proved to be a very good thing.

The first time I met Robyn, she'd come in as a referral from her primary physician, who was concerned that Robyn may be depressed as the result of a recent breakup. When asked, Robyn said that the breakup was her idea but that she was having a hard time getting over her ex. With that statement, she started to cry and continued to cry for the remainder of the session.

Hesitant to immediately diagnose her, I invited Robyn to start therapy with me so I could get to know her better and see the true extent of her symptoms. She agreed, and we began twice weekly sessions. At first she spoke mostly about the breakup and cried a lot, but as I got to know her better I realized that Robyn's weepiness was not depression; it was sadness and had more to do with her upbringing than her most recent relationship.

As we explored her family history and her relation-ship with her siblings, Robyn cried and cried. Each session was tearier than the last, and after she left each session, she headed straight to a drive-through. That's not unusual, by the way. Often when upsetting or unsettling material comes up in therapy, people eat to make it go away. Until they don't.

Eventually, Robyn stopped. She stopped crying, and she stopped the drive-throughs. She stopped because she finished feeling the sadness of her youth. Over time, she talked the issues out so that they no longer hurt her. When that happened, she no longer needed to eat to mask the pain. There was no more pain. Did we change the past? No, certainly not. But what we did do was deal with the past, release the past, and put the past to rest. As for the boyfriend whose breakup brought her into therapy, if you asked Robyn now she'd say, "What boyfriend?" He's a nonissue; that's for sure.

* * * * *

Jessie, a Case Study of Depression

Unlike Robyn's situation, which was amenable to weekly psychotherapy sessions to resolve, Jessie's was not. Jessie required three therapy sessions a week and medication to get started. Let me explain.

Jessie is a likeable bear of a man. He looks like a cross between Santa Claus and Paul Bunyan. At forty-two, Jessie was going through a serious loss. His wife of twelve years died of ovarian cancer, leaving him with their two children, Jessie Jr., age eleven, and Kaitlin, age nine. Jessie is a devoted father and loves his kids dearly. In true lumberjack spirit, he would be strong for his kids. But inside, he was a wreck.

I met Jessie when his wife was sick. He was referred to me by his wife's oncologist because she knew that he was having a hard time dealing with his wife's illness. In fact,

Jessie had gained fifty-five pounds since her diagnosis eighteen months earlier.

In the weeks after his wife's death, Jessie exhibited all the symptoms of a major depressive episode. In that condition, there really wasn't much we could do in weekly therapy sessions, so the first thing I did was refer him to a psychiatrist in my office building. She saw him immediately and put him on an antidepressant medication. Jessie and I then increased our therapy sessions to three times a week.

As the antidepressants did their work and Jessie's mood improved, he was able to do the grief work he desperately needed to. It took a few months, but Jessie made it through the stages of grief and was able to deal with his wife's passing and parenting their preadolescent kids very well. We cut our sessions back to once a week, then every other week, and then once a month.

Within a year, Jessie's weight returned to normal, and he and his kids were flourishing.

* * * * *

Is there anything about Robyn and her story that reflects you and your life? What about Jessie's? Are your feelings manageable or do you, like Jessie, need some extra care and support? Write what these stories bring up for you below.

About Me

_____

_____

_____

_____

_____

_____
_____
_____
_____
_____
_____
_____
_____
_____
_____
_____
_____
_____
_____
_____
_____
_____
_____
_____
_____
_____
_____
_____
_____
_____
_____
_____

Now that you have an idea of what *sadness* is and the role it may play in your eating habits, it's time to make a plan for what you will do to deal with sad feelings the next time they show up. Use the space below to write down your tactics and then rewrite them in your "My Emotional Obstacles Action

Plan." And remember, if what you are feeling is depression, take it seriously and seek professional help. Having the blues is one thing, but a diagnosable depression is something else.

Dealing with My Sadness Action Plan

The strategies I can employ to deal with *sadness* instead of eating are:

1.

2.

3.

4.

5.

Dealing with My Depression Action Plan

The strategies I can employ to deal with *depression* instead of eating are:

1.

2.

3.

4.

5.

CHAPTER ELEVEN

Stress and Tension

You have arrived—obstacle number eight. Congratulations! You have done a lot of excellent work. And by now, you are probably more confident about your ability to recognize your feelings and have some idea of what else you can do instead of eat over them. If you are ready, let's begin the eighth and final obstacle—stress and tension.

What Is Stress?

Stress is any situation (real or imagined) that threatens your sense of well-being. These situations can be divided into three categories—catastrophic occurrences, life-changing events, and daily-living hassles.

Stressful events that are considered *catastrophic occurrences* include terrorist attacks, plane crashes, tornados, hurricanes, earthquakes, and floods. These are disasters outside of your control that you have to contend with. Depending on their severity and impact, these incidents can lead to depression and anxiety.

For example, after 9/11, many people experienced symptoms of both these conditions. In fact, after the tragedy of that day, the "[consumption of] comfort food exploded" according to *Food & Wine* restaurant editor Kate Krader. She went on to say, "There is a kind of illogical need for stuff like macaroni and cheese, and fried chicken. Stuff that is not going to challenge you at all after a time when you've been really emotionally challenged. And you kind of just want to sit there and have a no-brainer dinner, or feel like someone's going to take care of you, like your mom" (as quoted on www.examiner.com).

She's correct. I saw the same effect in my clients. For a period of time, many increased their food intake until they'd worked through their feelings about that event. Fortunately for most of us, these experiences are rare and infrequent.

Significant *life-changing events* include illness, a divorce, and unemployment. It's understandable that these experiences would be stress inducing. Even positive life changes, such as marriage and a promotion, can lead to stress.

But possibly the most damaging type of stress is the stress that comes with everyday life. *Daily-living hassles* such as traffic jams, long lines, and job demands can really take their toll. Such stress, if prolonged, can become chronic, and chronic stress can negatively affect your health.

This is what the APA has to say about stress: "Stress can be a reaction to a short-lived situation, such as being stuck in traffic. Or it can last a long time if you're dealing with relationship problems, a spouse's death or other serious situations. Stress becomes dangerous when it interferes with your ability to live a normal life over an extended period. You may feel tired, unable to concentrate or irritable. Stress can also damage your physical health" (adapted from "Mind/Body: Stress" at www.apa.org).

What Is Tension?

As the APA says, stress can damage your health. Indeed, for many people, stress shows up physically in the form of tension. These people complain of aches and pains, stiffness and fatigue, insomnia, and stomach issues. I've also heard people complain about headaches and back spasms. It's not unusual for psychological matters to show up as physical complaints. Plenty of research supports the mind-body connection. So the notion that stress is felt physically as "tension" makes a lot of sense.

What Do Your Stress and Tension Look Like?

Now I'd like you to consider how you experience stress and tension. To get a better handle on this, here are some questions to get you thinking:

- What kind of things cause you stress?
- Are you upset by daily hassles or do you take them in stride but get derailed by the big issues?
- When you feel stressed, do you immediately turn to food?
  - o Have you ever tried anything else?
- Does your stress feel relentless, like a never-ending siege from which you can see no relief?
- How do you feel your stress?
  - o Headaches?
  - o Stomachaches?
  - o Joint pain?
  - o Neck pain?
- How would you define tension for yourself?

I have created a table for you to use to help you understand the role stress plays in your life. In this table, entitled "My Stressor Chart," list your stressors and mark whether each is a catastrophic occurrence, a life-changing event or a daily-living hassle. Then rank them in terms of how they affect you and your eating. Rank as number one the stress that affects your eating the most and work down from there. By doing so, you will become ready to find a way to deal with them and be able to leave food alone.

You will notice that the "My Stressor Chart" has a column called "My New Response." You can fill that in later once you have learned the skills you can use to manage your stress and tension.

My Stressor Chart

Stressor	Catastrophic	Life-Changing	Daily-Living	Rank	My New Response

What Can You Do When You Feel Stress or Tension?

By now, you are becoming familiar with cognitive therapy. That's the therapy that focuses on what you think. You learned a lot about this kind of therapy when we discussed anxiety and the anxious thoughts that create it.

Cognitive therapy has a sister. Her name is cognitive behavioral therapy, or CBT. CBT combines the thoughts you think with the actions you take. Today, cognitive behavioral therapy is very popular.

The answer to the question what can you do when you feel stress or tension is found in CBT. We will begin with two CBT strategies that focus on coping skills.

- *CBT Strategy # 1: Problem-Focused and Emotion-Focused Coping*
  In psychological circles, we talk about dealing with stress with coping skills that focus either on the problem itself or the emotions the stressful situation causes.

  The first is called problem-focused coping, and our attention is on the source of the stress and possible solutions.

  The other is known as emotion-focused coping. Here we acknowledge that we can't change the circumstances that are causing the stress, so instead, we deal with the emotions that they elicit.

  For example, your car has broken down again. This time, the mechanic tells you the repairs will cost a thousand dollars. Talk about stress. You are upset, angry, and worried. You become preoccupied with the situation, dwell on it, and can't stop thinking about it. When you use *problem-focused coping*, your attention will be on the cause of the stress and finding a remedy for it. So, if your car has broken down, your focus will be on getting it fixed. You would figure out how to find the money and the logistics surrounding the repair work.

On the other hand, when you use *emotion-focused coping*, you recognize that you can't change the situation; the only thing you can alter is your emotional reaction. So, in the case of your car breaking down, emotion-focused coping would mean that your attention is on how you are feeling and your efforts to calm yourself down.

Both approaches can work; you choose.

- *CBT Strategy # 2: Developing an Optimistic Explanatory Style*
  You can also deal with stress by changing how you explain things to yourself. A person can have an optimistic explanatory style or a pessimistic one. You know, "is the glass half-full or half-empty?" With respect to stressful situations, you can think of them in terms of challenges (optimistic) or threats (pessimistic).

  Using the example from above, you can use an *optimistic explanatory style* and tell yourself that the most recent car problem is a "challenge." In this case, you approach the problem with such ideas as (1) coming up with the money to pay for the repair, (2) finding another way to repair the car, or (3) using it as an opportunity to get a new car.

  On the other hand, if you tell yourself that your broken down car and the impending financial cost to repair it is (1) a huge dilemma, (2) a danger to your livelihood, or (3) the worst thing that could happen to you, you are using a *pessimistic explanatory style.* Perceiving the broken down car as a "threat" to your well-being leads to additional stress and tension.

The first approach, grounded in optimism, is empowering and exciting. The other, based in pessimism, is debilitating and defeating. The situation is the same. The difference is how you choose to perceive it.

To cope effectively with stress and tension, it is valuable to learn the optimistic explanatory style. It is possible for you to see the glass as half-full. To teach yourself how, read the following five steps:

Step 1: Identify a problem you need to explain to yourself.
Ex. I got a "C" on my midterm exam.

Step 2: Ask yourself, "What is good about this problem?" By asking this question, your mind will search for answers.
Ex. What is good about getting a "C" my midterm exam?

Step 3: Identify three answers to the question in Step 2.
Ex. Three good things about getting a "C" on my midterm exam are (1) I know what I don't know, (2) I know what works and what doesn't work when it comes to my study habits, and (3)I know what I need to do differently to get a higher score on my final exam.

Step 4: Redefine your problem in the form of a question.

Ex. What do I need to do to get an "A" on my final exam?

Step 5: List four possible solutions to the redefined problem.

Ex. Four solutions to my getting an "A" on my final exam are (1) starting to study earlier, (2) reading the chapters before class, (3) seeing the professor during office hours if I have questions, and (4) forming a study group with other students.

- *CBT Strategy #3: Social Support*

Being surrounded by loving and caring friends, family, coworkers, and neighbors can do wonders to help you cope. Research has shown us that social support is known to have curative effects for stress. Think about the people you have in your life who you can call upon when you need help. Reach out. If they are like most people, they want to help you. If you don't have anyone you can rely on, make finding such people a priority.

It may feel as if finding new people and making friends will require time and effort you don't seem to have. In truth, establishing healthy relationships is one the best things you can do for yourself, so I encourage you to find a way. It may not be as daunting a task as you think.

Simply look around you at the people who are already in your life and ask yourself if there is anyone with whom you cross paths who seems to you like a kind, caring person. If yes, take a risk and approach that person. Suggest a cup of coffee or a walk. You never know where your new BFF may come from.

Here's a list of people to consider:

- coworkers
- church or temple members
- people at the dog park
- the parents of your children's friends
- neighbors
- Zumba class participants
- players on your softball team
- guys at the local basketball pickup game

Identify some other people you could consider:

- _____
- _____
- _____
- _____
- _____

As Barbra Streisand once sang, "People who need people are the luckiest people in the world." Be lucky.

- *CBT Strategy #4: Meditation*
  Mindful Meditation is all the rage these days—and for good reason. It is an excellent tool for managing stress and relieving tension. Based in ancient traditions, meditation is very much a twenty-first century activity.

To meditate means to be still. It is not about quieting your mind because, quite frankly, that is impossible. It's about being with your mind and your thoughts in a peaceful way.

To mediate, what you need to do is find a quiet place where you will not be disturbed for a while. Turn off your phone and take a seat. Close your eyes and just be. Pay attention to your breathing. There is no need to change your breathing; just notice it. When thoughts pop into your mind, notice them but do not engage them. Let them pass through your mind like a puffy cloud on a crisp spring day. Do that for a few minutes, and you're done.

With practice, you will be able to sit for longer stretches of time. Eventually, you may be able to do twenty minutes twice a day.

In the resource section of this book, I list some meditation CDs you might enjoy.

- *CBT Strategy #5: More Stress-Reducing Activities*
  Keep in mind that people probably do more eating in response to stress and tension than to anything else. To overcome overeating, it is imperative that you learn other ways to cope with stress. Participating in regular stress-reducing activities is a good way to do just that. It is important to learn to manage your stress and keep it at bay. I often say that stress is like filling a glass with water. At first, there is plenty of room for the water, but after a while, the water starts to spill over if you have no way of removing it. If you cut a hole in the bottom of the glass and allowed water to drain out while still pouring water in, you could prevent the cup from overflowing.

It is the same with stress. Life causes all of us a certain amount of stress, and then stuff happens and it adds more. If you do nothing to drain the stress from your body, it, like the glass, will overflow.

To develop a stress management program of your own, begin by practicing the cognitive strategies described above, and then add on others.

Here are some ideas to get you started:

- Exercise:
    - Shoot hoops.
    - Dance.
    - Ride your bike.
    - Take a walk.
    - Go for a jog.
    - Stretch.
    - Go to the driving range and hit a bucket of balls.
- Relax:
    - Get a massage.
    - Listen to soothing music.
    - Practice relaxation techniques.
    - Practice deep breathing.
    - Stroke a pet.
    - Cradle a sleeping child.
    - Sip some herbal tea.
- Disengage for a while:
    - Turn off your phone and pager.
    - Stop checking Facebook, Twitter, and Instagram.
    - Put your iPod and iPad away.
    - Read.
    - Take a nap.

- Watch a good movie.
- Play a video game.

It is a welcome sight for me to see someone who was stressed out find peace without using food. Take Bianca as an example. At first she was very resistant to the idea of using meditation to deal with her stress and food issues. But in the end, she sure was glad she did. Maybe you will be too.

* * * * *

Bianca, a Case Study of Stress and Tension

Bianca was a bundle of nerves. At forty-two, she had a good life but could barely enjoy it because she was so easily overwhelmed by whatever was going on around her. She carried the weight of the world on her shoulders. Sandwiched between two college-aged kids; two aging parents, three if you included her mother-in-law; and a full-time job as a bookkeeper, Bianca ate all the time. It was her medicine. She nibbled sweets throughout the day. As a consequence, her weight was going up and up, which only added to the negative feelings she was burdened with.

One day, I recommended that Bianca meditate. I educated her on the benefits to her emotional and physical well-being of quieting her mind through meditation, and she laughed at me. She laughed because she couldn't imagine finding the time to meditate, never mind being able to silence the chatter in her head. I explained that all she needed to do was sit for five minutes and focus on her breathing. That's it. No bells, no whistles, no gongs. She couldn't believe that something so minimal could be beneficial, but I convinced her to give it a try.

The first week, she managed to sit two times for five minutes. She kept at it, and after about six weeks, she was taking ten minutes a day to focus on her breathing.

Something interesting happened around that time. Bianca's younger son broke his leg and had to come home from college to recover. In the past, this added stress would have sent Bianca straight into a box of chocolate chip cookies. But not this time. This time, she didn't even think about the cookies.

When I pointed this out to her, she was surprised. What happened? Easy. The daily meditation sessions were reducing her overall stress levels so that, when the new stress was added on, she was able to cope without needing to turn to food. That was all Bianca had to hear.

Meditation became a regular practice, such that she increased her daily sessions to twenty minutes twice a day. Over the course of the next year, her weight dropped by almost forty pounds. If you asked her, she would say it was a "miracle." To me, it was good stress management habits in action.

* * * * *

Are you looking for a "miracle?" What good stress management habits can you add to your life to bring about the changes you want? Record your ideas below, keeping in mind what you might want to include in your "Stress and Tension Action Plan." Review this list to get your wheels turning:

- meditate
- exercise
- dance
- take a walk

- go for a jog
- stretch
- get a massage
- listen to soothing music
- read
- practice relaxation techniques
- take some deep breaths
- stroke a pet
- cradle a sleeping child
- sip some herbal tea
- turn off your phone and laptop

About Me

_____

_____

_____

_____

_____

_____

_____

_____

_____

_____

_____

_____

_____

_____

_____

_____

_____

_____

_____

_____

_____

_____

_____

_____

_____

_____

_____

_____

Now that you have an idea of what *stress* and *tension* are and the role they may play in your eating habits, it's time to make a plan for managing them. Use the space below to write down your approach and then transfer your ideas to the "My Emotional Obstacles Action Plan." Try to do something every day to keep your stress under control. Even a simple walk can do wonders to keep you out of the fridge.

Dealing with My Stress and Tension Action Plan

The strategies I can employ to deal with *stress* and *tension* instead of eating are:

1.

2.

3.

4.

5.

CHAPTER TWELVE

Achieving Your Ideal Weight

Hi. You made it to Chapter Twelve. Or did you start here? Either way, welcome. If you've being reading along, you know by now that the key to a successful and long-lasting experience on any food plan is managing your emotions. You've just completed a crash course in identifying, understanding, and coping with the eight emotional obstacles to weight loss. So now what to you do?

Simple—you apply what you've learned. Not once. Not for a week. But for a lifetime. Practice what you have learned here until doing so is second nature. Once you have these habits well-established, you won't have to worry about your emotions hijacking your weight anymore.

Keep in mind that this process is not a magic fix. It will take time for your body to reflect your efforts. Please try to judge your success not by the numbers on the scale or the size of your jeans but, rather, by how your relationship to food is improving. If you keep to your healthy eating and exercise plans and manage your emotions effectively, over time, you will see results.

(One caveat: If after a reasonable amount of time following your diet and exercise plans and practicing the coping skills suggested in this book you are not seeing any weight loss, I would like to encourage you to review your efforts with your physician. Some medical conditions [thyroid conditions, medication side effects, and hormonal fluctuations, for example] can interfere with weight loss. Your physician can help you discern if you have a problem and then recommend additional steps you can take to reach your goals.)

In a nutshell, here's what you do:

1. Identify the feelings you are experiencing.
   a. Anger?
   b. Boredom/emptiness?
   c. Deprivation?
      i. Food deprivation?
      ii. Loss deprivation?
   a. Fear/anxiety?
   b. Hopelessness?
   c. Loneliness?
   d. Sadness/depression?
   e. Stress/tension?
2. Give yourself permission to have the feelings.
3. Find a quiet place where you can be alone with your feelings.
4. Once you are alone, sit down and simply be with your feelings.
5. Feel all aspects of your feelings—body and mind.
6. As the feelings start to pass, consider the options you have to handle the cause of the feelings. Some examples include:
   a. The Tip Sheets found in chapter thirteen
   b. The skills and techniques described in chapter fourteen

    c.   Your "Emotional Obstacles Action Plan" if you created one

7.   Pick one of those options.

8.   Do it.

That's it. Simple. Keep practicing and you'll get good at dealing with your emotions without overeating.

One way to know how well you are doing is to give yourself credit. Specifically, use the "Self-Credit Chart." Each day, make a note indicating something you did (or didn't do) that was good for you. For example, eating a healthy meal, walking instead of driving, saying no instead of yes, expressing your anger instead of eating over it.

Feel free to make copies of the checklist so you can have it handy. I have included some sample entries to show you how to use this resource.

Self-Credit Chart – Sample

Day	Emotions Success	Food Plan Success	Exercise Success	Other Successes
Monday	Called my sister when upset over supervisor's remark	Ate a salad with my sandwich instead of fries at lunch today	Took twenty-minute walk after dinner with husband instead of watching TV	Been practicing mediation for two weeks now – Up to five minutes a day.
Tuesday	Took a ten-minute break before telling John how mad I was	Ordered a light beer at dinner – saved 150 calories	Played racket ball with Stu for an hour at lunch time; Won!	My girlfriend tells me I am a better communicator since I started this process

Self-Credit Chart

Day	Emotions Success	Food Plan Success	Exercise Success	Other Successes

In addition, it helps to acknowledge your strengths and to draw upon them when you are faltering.

You may be thinking that you have no strengths, but I assure you, you do. Here is a list of ten common strengths. Check off the ones that apply to you. Add others that you think of.

Strengths Checklist

- ✓ commitment
- ✓ compassion
- ✓ focus
- ✓ honesty

✓ loyalty
✓ persistence
✓ punctuality
✓ sense of humor
✓ tenacity
✓ willingness
✓ _____
✓ _____
✓ _____
✓ _____

With all the changes you have been making and the ideas you have been trying out, you can keep track of your efforts in the space below. Make some notes about what is working and what isn't, what you would like to try, and when you'd like to try it.

About Me

_____
_____
_____
_____
_____
_____
_____
_____
_____
_____
_____
_____
_____
_____

CHAPTER THIRTEEN

Tip Sheets

Welcome to the tip sheet chapter. I have created tip sheets for you to use on a daily basis to assist you in dealing with your life without turning to food to cope. Think of them as "cheat sheets." You are welcome to make copies of them so you can carry them with you, add to them, or post them as reminders of what else you can do instead of eating to deal with your feelings.

The first one, "101 Ways to Deal with Your Emotions without Eating," is adapted from my books *Self-Fullness: The Art of Loving and Caring for Your "Self"* and *Do You Use Food to Cope? A Comprehensive 15-Week Program for Overcoming Emotional Overeating.* This tip sheet lists different feelings and circumstances that might send you looking to food for comfort. Instead, look through the list for the topic that matches the position you find yourself in and do one of the suggested activities.

101 Ways to Deal with Your Emotions without Eating

Are You Angry?
1. Understand what you are angry about.
2. Express your anger constructively by writing or speaking about it.
3. Hit a pillow.
4. Beat your mattress up with a tennis racket or golf club.

Are You Angry with Someone in Particular?
5. Write his or her name on the bottom of your shoe in chalk and take a power walk.
6. Talk to the person with whom you are angry.

Feeling Frustrated?
7. Figure out the source of your woes and confront them. State your position clearly and assertively.

Feeling Bored?
8. Make a list of activities that you enjoy and then do one.

Are You Empty? Want to Make Your Life More Interesting?
9. Take up a hobby.
10. Get a part-time job.
11. Volunteer.
12. Join a book club.
13. Go back to school.
14. Learn a new language.
15. Learn to dance.
16. Train for a marathon.

Feeling Afraid or Anxious?

17. Get some physical exercise.
18. Eliminate caffeine, alcohol, and sugar from your diet.

Feeling Lonely?

19. Call a friend.
20. Adopt a pet.
21. Write a letter.
22. Join a group.
23. Take a class.

Feeling Sad or Depressed?

24. Identify why you are "down in the dumps."
25. Describe your feelings in words or pictures.
26. Talk it over with a friend, a family member, or a psychologist.

Feeling Stressed Out?

27. Practice relaxation.
28. Go for a walk.
29. Meditate.
30. Listen to music.
31. Go to a quiet place, reduce distractions, rest.

Feeling Tired?

32. Take a nap.
33. Do some exercise.

Can't Sleep?

34. Read a magazine.
35. Drink some soothing chamomile tea.

Is Your Body Aching?

36. Soak in a tub of Epsom salts.
37. Get a massage.
38. Stretch.

Need to Experience Your Feelings?

39. Sit with your feelings.
40. Give your feelings a name—sadness, fear, joy, worry.
41. Allow your feeling time to pass.
42. Let them move freely through your body without resistance.
43. Write your feelings in a letter or journal.
44. Talk to a friend or counselor.
45. Have a good cry.

Want to Develop a Positive Mental Attitude?

46. Practice positive self-talk.
47. Write several affirmations you can use daily.
48. Post your affirmations where you can see them.
49. Get an inspirational book and read it.
50. Get an inspirational calendar and hang it nearby.
51. Hang out with positive people.

Need Some Nurturing?

52. Get some R&R.
53. Soak in a Jacuzzi.
54. Warm up in a sauna.
55. Visit the steam room at your local YMCA.
56. Listen to soothing music.
57. Practice creative visualization.
58. Breathe deeply.
59. Do yoga.
60. Pet your dog.

61. Stroke your cat.
62. Get a hug.
63. Buy yourself a little something special.
64. Putter around in your garden.
65. Fill your favorite vase with fresh flowers.
66. Go to a spa for a manicure, pedicure, or facial.
67. Meet a buddy for some "guy time."
68. Try a new hairstyle.
69. Use your hands to repair or build something.
70. Watch a comedy on TV.

Need a Time-Out?

71. Read a good book.
72. Go to the movies.
73. Rent a video.
74. Call a friend long distance.
75. Take a drive.
76. Clean out a closet.
77. Clean out a drawer.
78. Dance to some music.
79. Do a crossword puzzle.
80. Skim a magazine.
81. Play a board game.
82. Go window-shopping.
83. Listen to a book on tape.
84. Prune your roses.
85. Plant some flowers.
86. Work on a jigsaw puzzle.
87. Play with the computer.
88. Go online.
89. Take a catnap.
90. Paint a picture.

Need Some New Skills?

91. Practice saying *no.*
92. Practice being assertive.
93. Make eye contact with someone.
94. Develop your intuition.
95. Ask yourself what you need.
96. Give yourself what you need.
97. Tell someone you love that you love him or her.
98. Take a class in something totally different.
99. Do something you have been putting off.
100. Find a mentor.
101. Read *Self-Fullness: The Art of Loving and Caring for Your "Self."*

40 Things to Do Instead of Giving in to a Craving

When you first stop using food as a way to assuage your emotions, you may find yourself at the mercy of cravings. The good news is food cravings pass if you let them. It usually takes about twenty minutes for that to happen, so distract yourself with one of these suggestions (or make up some of your own) and let the time fly:

1. Take a bath or shower.
2. Shave.
3. Soak your feet.
4. Get on a treadmill.
5. Do an exercise video.
6. Do laundry.
7. Iron clothes.
8. Run an errand (go to the dry cleaners, for example).
9. Run the dishwasher.

10. Mend an item or fix something.
11. Go for a walk.
12. Polish your shoes.
13. Water plants.
14. Sweep the patio.
15. Vacuum.
16. Check your e-mail.
17. Go for a drive.
18. Get your car washed.
19. Recycle.
20. Tear out pages of a magazine.
21. Throw out the garbage.
22. Organize—clean a drawer or closet or file.
23. Dust.
24. Take pictures.
25. Dance.
26. Brush your teeth.
27. Build something.
28. Give yourself a facial.
29. Put cream on your hands, feet, or cuticles.
30. Walk around a bookstore.
31. Take a nap.
32. Watch TV, a DVD, or a movie.
33. Brush the dog, pet the cat, or feed the fish.
34. Clean leather furniture or jacket.
35. Go to a drugstore for missing items.
36. Go to the library, get a book on something you know nothing about, and read it.
37. Go to the park.
38. Change clothes.
39. Put on makeup or shave.
40. Check your voice mail, and return calls.

35 Ways to Comfort Yourself

Eating for emotional reasons is really eating for comfort. You are feeling uneasy because of the emotion being felt and you use food to soothe it away. This is learned behavior. When you were little and skinned your knee and got a lollipop so you would stop crying, you were "taught" to use food to comfort yourself.

Not all comfort eating is bad. Even naturally thin people for whom food is neutral will dig into a carton of ice cream after a tough day. The difference is they do that form of self-soothing occasionally, not as a regular routine.

Now as an adult, whenever you feel as if you need some comfort food, you can choose one of these soothing activities instead. The more often you choose one of these other activities, the more quickly you will reach and stay at your ideal weight.

1. Take a walk.
2. Have a good cry.
3. Go to the barber for an old-fashioned shave and haircut.
4. Get a manicure/pedicure.
5. Shower, dress up, and go out.
6. Read inspirational books—get a new one.
7. Talk to God or any higher power you believe in— pray, ask, converse.
8. Set some goals.
9. Organize something that needs organizing.
10. Toss something that needs tossing.
11. Create a vision board (a collage of pictures, words, and images that reflect your dreams and goals).
12. Sit quietly and sip calming herbal tea.

13. Go for a drive.
14. Write in a journal.
15. Go to the movies.
16. Window-shop.
17. Sign up for a class in something new and different.
18. Take a bath (with essential oils).
19. Hug yourself or ask for a hug.
20. Get makeup done at a cosmetics counter.
21. Meditate/visualize.
22. Watch something funny—laugh.
23. Exercise (stretch, dance, or go to the gym).
24. Take a hot shower.
25. Buy yourself some flowers.
26. Schedule (or get) a massage.
27. Drink some water.
28. Identify your feelings, feel them, and address the real need they reveal.
29. Go to sleep early.
30. Buy yourself new, cozy, comfy pajamas or sweatpants.
31. Watch TV or a DVD.
32. Listen to music.
33. Go to the hair salon for a shampoo and blow-dry.
34. Walk around a bookstore.
35. Plan a trip somewhere exciting.

CHAPTER FOURTEEN

Using Your Imagination to Help Yourself

Our imaginations are incredible tools. I often say that worry and anxiety are manifestation of an imagination focused on the negative. If you harness your imaginative powers for good, there is nothing you can't achieve. So, use your imagination to help you along this journey. Since the imagination experiences things in the form of images, fill your mind with images of what you would like to see happen or would like to achieve. To do that, all you have to do is close your eyes, get yourself into a relaxed state of mind, and start imagining.

To get you going I've included a few sample visualizations for you to use. Feel free to adapt them to meet your specific needs and goals.

Surviving Holiday Parties Visualization

Close your eyes and get into a relaxed state of mind and body. Think about the particular holiday you are anticipating. Imagine all the foods you associate with that holiday. Now consider the idea that there will always be holidays. Imagine a calendar. Turn its pages and notice all the holidays, birthdays, anniversaries, and dinner parties. There will always be more. Each one could be time for you to slip off your plan. Think about how sad that idea is—how all your hard work will slip away.

Instead, think about new ways to celebrate that holiday. Think about how great you will feel if, on this holiday, you choose to do things differently. You choose to eat differently, exercise differently, or choose different activities. This holiday is a chance to discover what works for you. They're about different pleasures (like fitting into a smaller size) that are more satisfying than eating the same old food available at this holiday.

Enjoy discovering new ways of being on this holiday. Imagine yourself saying no to excess food. Visualize yourself having a new and better experience, one that leaves you feeling slim, healthy, and great about yourself. Luxuriate in this feeling for as long as you want.

When you are ready, open your eyes and enjoy the holiday, knowing that, this time, you will succeed in sticking with your plan and feeling good about what you did.

Dealing with Cravings Visualization

Close your eyes and get into a relaxed state of mind and body. Feel the craving or urge inside your body. Notice where it is. Pay attention to what it feels like. Is it static or does it move? What color is it? Hear what it is telling you. Listen to it. What is it really saying? What emotional need is it trying to communicate?

Talk to it. Tell it that you know it is there but that you are choosing to let it pass. Remind yourself that cravings pass. Imagine a few minutes passing and the craving no longer being present. Feel what that feels like in your body. Let yourself feel joy at the idea that the craving has passed. Think about what you will do next now that the craving has passed. See yourself doing that. See yourself going on with your life without having given in to your craving. Imagine how great you feel about yourself, your body, and your actions. Let these feelings wash over you.

When you are ready, open your eyes and enjoy knowing that, this time, you succeeded in letting a craving pass and feel good about what you have accomplished.

My Ideal Body Visualization

Close your eyes and get into a relaxed state of mind and body. Using all your senses, image yourself at your ideal weight, living in your ideal body. First, see yourself at your ideal weight. Imagine yourself at your ideal size. See yourself wearing your ideal clothes. Feel the texture of the clothes on your body. Admire yourself in a mirror. Touch your body. Feel its soft, smooth skin. Touch your slim face.

Now hear compliments. Imagine people telling you how great you look. Smile and say thank you. Let the compliments soak in. You've earned them. You are at your ideal weight.

Now see yourself engaged in a variety of activities. Go for a run or a walk. Take a swim. Choose whatever activities feel right for you. Experience yourself in those settings. See what you might see. Hear what you might hear. Smell what you might smell. Take it all in and appreciate how great everything feels to you now that you are at your ideal weight.

When you are ready open your eyes. Enjoy your magnificent body and feel good about what you have accomplished.

Perfect Food Shopping Trip Visualization

Close your eyes and get into a relaxed state of mind and body. Imagine yourself at the front door of your favorite supermarket. Your hands are on the handle of a shopping cart, and you are getting ready to enter. Stand there for a moment thinking about the healthy, delicious foods that you would like to fill your cart with.

As you walk into the store, take in all the beautiful colors around you. Notice the bright yellow of the bananas and the red of the apples. Next, take a deep inhale and smell the freshly baked, whole grain breads wafting from the bakery and the aroma of the rotisserie chicken coming from the deli. See yourself walking the perimeter of the store and loading your cart with the most delicious fresh fruits and vegetables, the leanest cuts of meat and poultry, wild caught seafood, and lots of organic dairy. As you fill your cart, notice how good you are feeling about yourself and your choices. Imagine the mouth-watering salad you will make for lunch and the sautéed vegetable and poached salmon you will prepare for dinner.

Walk over to the cashier and put your items on the conveyor belt. As you place each item down, you notice how proud you are about the purchases you are making and how well you are taking care of yourself. Smile. You've done a great job shopping today. Now you can go home and enjoy your choices.

When you are ready, open your eyes and enjoy knowing that, this time, you succeeded in shopping for healthy, nutritious foods and feel good about what you have accomplished.

Perfect Restaurant Dining Visualization

Close your eyes and get into a relaxed state of mind and body. It's time for dinner at your favorite restaurant. In anticipation of coming here today, you dressed up. You did your hair and put on a favorite outfit. You look and feel good and are ready to have a wonderful dining experience that will nourish you in body, mind, and spirit.

You are led to your table, and you sit down. Take in the surroundings. Notice the tablecloths and dishes. Pay attention to the sights and smells. As the waiter hands you the menu, think for a moment about what you would like to eat that would be delicious and would also support you in your efforts to be healthy and lean.

Open the menu and peruse the choices. Your eyes settle on one particular dish that would meet your intention. Tell the waiter that you will have that dish. The waiter acknowledges your good choice. As you wait for the dish to arrive, take a moment to give yourself credit for your choice. You have done a good thing for yourself. Feel good about it.

The waiter comes with your dish. He places it in front of you. You look at the dish and give thanks for it. Lift up your fork and slip it into your mouth. For a moment, let the food sit on your tongue. Notice its flavors. Feel its texture. Now chew it, enjoying every morsel. Eat this dish slowly and mindfully. Recognize its value to you in both taste and health. When you are finished, place your fork across the plate and give thanks for the delicious meal.

When you are ready, open your eyes and enjoy knowing that, this time, you succeeded in having a delicious meal at your favorite restaurant and feel good about what you have accomplished.

Joyful Exercise Visualization

Close your eyes and get into a relaxed state of mind and body. Now it is time to exercise. Think about a particular kind of exercise that you would like to partake in. Imagine yourself dressed for that exercise. Enter the area where you will be exercising. It could be a health club, your living room, or the great outdoors. Take moment and experience this location with all your senses. Look around to see what you see. Take a deep breath and inhale the aroma. Listen closely to the sounds around you. Touch something and feel its texture. Perhaps it is your shoelace or a towel or dumbbell.

Next, put a smile on your face and begin your movements. Imagine yourself doing the exercising flawlessly. If it is a Zumba class you are taking, imagine swinging your hips from side to side with ease. If you are running, feel the wind in your hair and the light tapping of your feet on the sidewalk. Spend a few minutes imaging yourself doing your exercise and enjoying every moment of it. See yourself as an athlete performing your moves with skill and ease. And most importantly, be happy. Feel your body growing stronger and leaner with each move. Feel your power and endurance. You are getting into better shape with each action, and you love it.

Start to wind down your exercise. Imagine yourself wiping the sweat from your brow and sipping some refreshing, cool water. Stretch your body and feel how limber you are now.

When you are ready, open your eyes and enjoy knowing that, this time, you succeeded in moving your body and engaging in joyful exercise and feel good about what you have accomplished.

Healthy Eating at Home Visualization

Close your eyes and get into a relaxed state of mind and body. See yourself in your kitchen or dining room. Imagine a beautifully set table complete with pretty dishes, nice glassware, and stemware. Put some fresh flowers on the table, and if you want to, light some candles. Take a plate and fill it with the most delicious, healthy food—a large green salad perhaps or maybe a big bowl of steamed vegetables over rice, whatever you prefer.

Place the plate in front of you and sit down. Take a good look at your plate and notice all the colors. Appreciate nature's bounty that is in front of you. Notice the aromas it emits. Take a forkful and imagine taking a bite. Feel the textures. Taste the tastes. Savor each morsel. Slowly eat the food you have prepared and pay close attention to the health benefits each bite provides. Remind yourself that the food you are eating is not only delicious, it is good for you. Take your time and enjoy your meal.

When you are ready, open your eyes knowing that, this time, you succeeded in eating a healthy meal at home and feel good about what you have accomplished.

* * * * *

I hope you found these visualizations helpful and relevant to your life. If you want, you can try your hand at creating one specifically for you. Use the space below to do just that. Have fun.

About Me

_____

_____

_____

_____

_____

_____

_____

More Success Tools

Here are some additional tools you can use. Look them over and practice them. Keep your favorites in mind for the next time you are tempted by emotional hunger.

Sixty-Second Images

Whenever you are in a tight spot, take a minute to close your eyes, relax your mind and body, and think about something that will get you through the moment. For example, imagine yourself

- wearing a smaller size;
- making a healthy food choice;
- being at the beach in a bathing suit and feeling wonderful about your body;
- saying no to a food that is not on your plan;
- seeing your goal weight on the scale;
- exercising with joy;
- making a grand entrance and turning heads as you do;
- where you want to be in a year;
- enjoying other activities with family and friends;
- at your goal weight;
- effortlessly staying on your food plan;
- at your very best;
- doing your very best;
- feeling great about yourself;
- feeling proud about yourself;
- having mastery over your emotions; or
- having mastery over your eating habits.

Add your own *Sixty-Second Images* here:

-

-

-

-

-

Self-Talkies

Earlier in this book, I talked with you about the role your thoughts play in how you feel. For example, thoughts fraught with worry will leave you anxious. Affirming thoughts will help get you through your day. Based on cognitive therapy, this tool is designed to improve your inner dialogue by teaching you to use positive self-talk statements to keep yourself on track. You can say them aloud or silently, whatever works for you when you need them.

Here are some you can try:

- I know the difference between physical and emotional hunger, and I only eat when I am physically hungry.
- Cravings pass when I turn my attention away from them.
- My old habits are dying off.
- My new habits are gaining strength.

- I can do this.
- I am doing this.
- Every day, I am getting better at handling my food.
- I can stay on my plan.
- I can exercise.
- I don't have to give into a craving.
- I don't have to give into an urge to eat.
- I address my emotions directly.
- I am no longer at the mercy of my appetite.
- I am no longer at the mercy of my cravings.
- I am free to have the life I want.
- I am free to have the body I want.
- I am free to have excellent health.
- I can let cravings pass.
- I deserve a great life.
- I deserve a great body.
- I deserve a healthy body.
- I deserve to be at peace with food.
- I want my goal more than I want excess food.

Add your own *Self-Talkies* here:

-

-

-

-

-

Negative Consequences

I know you can tell I'm a big believer in focusing on the positive rather than the negative. However, it can be helpful to remind yourself of what the negative consequences could be if you choose to overeat rather than confront your emotions. Sometimes a quick review of such consequences is enough to move you in a different direction.

Here are some examples of such consequences:

- I will continue to have low self-esteem.
- My body image will be bad.
- I will add excess weight to my frame.
- I will have to wear big sizes.
- My health will suffer.
- I will experience self-loathing.
- My relationships will be damaged.
- My problem will still exist, and I'll be fatter.
- I'll stay stuck instead of moving forward.

Use these "reminders" when you are feeling a bit wobbly in your efforts to move forward in this journey. Don't dwell on them. Simple take a moment to reflect on them if doing so will inch you in the direction you really want to go.

You can use the ones I listed above or you can list your own *Negative Consequences* here:

-
-
-
-

Going for the Good

You may have heard over and over again to think positively. You may be familiar with affirmations and the idea that, if you repeat these positive statements to yourself overtime, you will experience their benefits. While I have nothing against positive thinking and affirmations—they are valuable tools for coping with emotional distress—I find that many people struggle with them. When you are in a state of distress, it may be hard to come up with something positive to say or think. Or when you do but you don't believe what you are saying or thinking, your efforts to use these tools could be short-lived.

I have another suggestion. Instead of looking for the positive in a situation, turn your attention to the good that is already in your life. Let me explain.

When you are feeling upset over a particular situation, it is often hard to "see the bright side." Let's say you just got a letter from the IRS saying you are going to be audited. Anyone in that situation would feel nervous and overwhelmed. Being told to think positively about such an audit is a hard thing to do. Being told to look at the bright side can seem like a pretty dim suggestion.

So, what can you do? You can stop and think about what good you do have in your life right now. Will thinking about the good in your life change the fact that there is an audit in your future? No, but what it can do is improve your mood, which in turn can make it easier for you to deal with the upcoming audit.

Here's what you do. Offer ten answers to this question and follow each answer with the phrase, "That's good."

Question: *What is good in my life right now?*

How about:

1. I found a parking spot easily today. That's good.
2. My last paycheck cleared without any hassle. That's good.
3. It's not raining. That's good.
4. Or (if you are in draught-stricken Southern California) it is raining. That's good.
5. My kids are healthy. That's good.
6. My car alarm isn't ringing. That's good.
7. I have hot water to take a shower in. That's good.
8. My favorite TV show is on tonight. That's good.
9. The library has the book I want. That's good.
10. I like the color our house is painted. That's good.

Are you starting to see how this works? None of these statements have anything to do with the audit. But they are truths about your life. The more you focus on what is good, the better you will feel. As you get used to doing this exercise, change it to, "That's great." You'll notice that you feel even better.

Now, it's your turn.

Describe the situation that has you bummed out: _____

_____
_____
_____
_____
_____
_____
_____
_____

Now write down ten answers to the question, *What is good in my life right now?* And follow each answer with the phrase "That's good."

1. _____
   _____

2. _____
   _____

3. _____
   _____

4. _____
   _____

5. _____
   _____

6. _____
   _____

7. _____
   _____

8. _____
   _____

9. _____
   _____

10. _____
    _____

How are you feeling? Any better? If not, try ten more. Keep doing this until you notice a shift in your mood. With time, you may discover that this exercise is your favorite go-to tool for dealing with emotional distress.

These tools and techniques are here for you to use as needed as you continue to address your emotions without food. There may be some you use regularly and others you ignore. It may be helpful to revisit this chapter from time to time to see if a particular tool catches your attention. You can use the "About Me" section that follows to make note of any tools that you might like to give a try.

About Me

_____

_____

_____

_____

_____

_____

_____

_____

_____

_____

_____

_____

_____

_____

_____

_____

_____

_____

_____

_____

CHAPTER SIXTEEN

Weight Loss That Lasts: Staying Motivated

Equally important to getting the weight off is keeping it off—for good. Once you have arrived at your ideal weight, it takes effort and dedication to stay there. It may be easy to stay committed to practicing new habits while you are losing weight, but once your weight stabilizes, motivation can wane. Since reverting back to old habits can undo all your hard work, let's take some time to address motivation.

What Is Motivation?

Motivation is the energy that drives you toward a goal. It's the idea, thing, or feeling that makes the goal worth the effort. Ask any Olympic athlete, and I'm sure he or she will tell you that thinking about standing on the podium with a gold medal hanging around his or her neck while the national anthem plays in the background makes getting up at five o'clock for a training session easier.

What Does Motivation Feel Like?

Motivation feels different for each of us. For some, it is a surge of energy pulsing through their veins. For others, it's a restlessness—an eagerness to get moving or started or finished.

What does motivation feel like for you?

What Motivates You?

Some people are motivated by achievement. Having a sense of accomplishment is all they need to make an action "non-negotiable." Then there are those who are motivated by rewards—a prize of some sort, whether it is a gold medal or a hundred bucks.

Think about what motivates you. Does the idea of a reward appeal to you? If yes, then consider rewarding yourself at specific intervals or for the completion of a particular task. For example, how about a Swedish massage for staying on your food plan over a holiday weekend? Or a new novel after you finishing reading this book? You get the idea.

What Can You Do to Motivate Yourself?

In psychology, we talk about using *positive reinforcements* when we want to strengthen or increase a desired behavior. As a university professor, I gave my students either candy or stickers each time they read a chapter before class. I did this to encourage them to read the textbook.

Positive reinforcements can be offered at regular intervals, like each week in class after reading the textbook, or after specific tasks, such as for every ten pounds lost.

How could you use positive reinforcements to encourage

the new habits you are trying to instill? And, how can you use positive reinforcement to keep those habits in place for the long haul?

* * * * *

Alex, a Case Study of Motivation

One of the best examples I have of a person staying motivated and committed to his weight loss and beyond comes from my patient, Alex. Alex is a package delivery man—you know, those cute guys in the shorts who deliver packages to your front door. Alex was one of them. And Alex was cute, despite weighing over three hundred pounds.

Alex came to see me after his wife met me at a talk I gave on the relationship between emotions and weight. She was worried that Alex had gained a lot of weight since his father died. She felt he wasn't dealing with this loss and was eating instead. I offered Alex a free consultation, and he took me up on it.

Within minutes, I could see that Alex's wife was right. Alex was eating over the death of his father, instead of dealing with it. Alex agreed to twice a week therapy and hired a personal trainer. He wasn't interested in going on a plan but agreed to exercise and follow some common sense advice about food choices and portion sizes.

At first, Alex resisted talking about his father. But eventually, he opened up. It took about three months for Alex to work through his feelings over his father's death. During that time, he continued with his personal training and had lost over twenty pounds.

We were nearing the end of our therapy when Alex's wife announced she was pregnant with their first child. Alex was ecstatic about becoming a father. Rather than end therapy, Alex was motivated to continue learning about both his emotions and health and fitness. Alex's father had died at fifty-seven from a heart attack, and now that he was about to be a father, he didn't want that same thing to happen to his children.

Alex's commitment to his wife and his unborn child carried him through the next nine months of healthy eating, working out, and therapy. By the time his son, Henry, was born, Alex had lost one hundred pounds and was in the best condition of his life.

Alex continued therapy and working out with his trainer after Henry was born. It is now four years later, and Alex is still fit, trim, and healthy. He told me recently that he has no intention of stopping what he has been doing. He said to me, "Doc, you were right. My old way of living made me fat and sick, and my new way is keeping me young and fit." Those words were music to my ears.

* * * * *

Think about motivation and the role it could play in achieving your permanent weight-loss goals. Record your ideas here.

About Me

_____

_____

_____

_____

_____

_____

Some Bottom Line Advice

Now that you have taken a look at your emotions and how they can get in the way of your achieving your weight-loss goals, you are on your way to making changes to how you cope with your emotions so you can stick to your food and exercise plans. Doing that will lead you to weight loss that lasts. The key is to just start.

Dealing with your emotions without using food to cope will be a lifelong habit. You don't have to be perfect at it, just consistent. Keep practicing recognizing your emotions and finding new and better ways to express them, and you'll find that, over time, these new patterns of behavior will become habits and your weight will get to and stay where it belongs. As I have said before, remember, this is a process, and making these changes takes time.

If you have been reading carefully and thinking about what you are learning, then what I am about to share will not come as a surprise to you. To overcome the emotional obstacles to permanent weight loss, you need to feel your feelings instead of feed your feelings. It is really that basic. Using food to avoid any emotion—happy or sad, exciting or frightening—will lead to excess weight every time. *But* when you learn to identify your feelings and choose to face them head-on, you will not consume unnecessary calories, and your weight will return to and stay at the weight that is right for you. So whether you choose to sit with your feelings until they pass or take constructive action to cope with them, you will find the success you seek. There is no secret—only effort and hard work.

I wish you the very best of luck as you travel this path. I am confident that, as you get more comfortable with your emotional life, your weight will take care of itself.

My Emotional Obstacles Action Plan

Below you will find space to record the actions you plan to take for each emotional obstacle. If you haven't already done so, please fill them in. You are welcome to make copies of this appendix so you can add to it, amend it, or delete items as you see fit.

The strategies I can employ to deal with *anger* instead of eating are:

1.

2.

3.

4.

5.

The strategies I can employ to deal with *boredom* instead of eating are:

1.

2.

3.

4.

5.

The strategies I can employ to deal with *emptiness* instead of eating are:

1.

2.

3.

4.

5.

The strategies I can employ to deal with *deprivation* instead of eating are:

1.

2.

3.

4.

5.

The strategies I can employ to deal with *fear* instead of eating are:

1.

2.

3.

4.

5.

The strategies I can employ to deal with *anxiety* instead of eating are:

1.

2.

3.

4.

5.

The strategies I can employ to deal with *hopelessness* instead of eating are:

1.

2.

3.

4.

5.

The strategies I can employ to deal with *loneliness* instead of eating are:

1.

2.

3.

4.

5.

The strategies I can employ to deal with *sadness* instead of eating are:

1.

2.

3.

4.

5.

The strategies I can employ to deal with *depression* instead of eating are:

1.

2.

3.

4.

5.

The strategies I can employ to deal with *stress* and *tension* instead of eating are:

1.

2.

3.

4.

5.

Suggested Resource List

If you are interested in learning more about the relationship between your emotions and your eating habits and how you can help yourself, I encourage you to check out these additional resources.

Books

Forman, Sheila H., JD, PhD, *Do You Use Food to Cope? A Comprehensive 15-Week Program for Overcoming Emotional Overeating* (Writers Club Press, 2002).

Taitz, Jennifer L., PsyD *End Emotional Eating* (New Harbinger Publications, Inc., 2012).

Normandi, Carol Emery and Laurelee Roark. *It's Not About Food* (The Berkley Publishing Group, 1998).

Spangle, Linda, RN, MA. *Life is Hard Food Is Easy.* (LifeLine Press, 2003).

Fairburn, Christopher. *Overcoming Binge Eating* (The Guilford Press, 1995).

Forman, Sheila H., JD, PhD. *Self-Fullness: The Art of Loving and Caring for Your "Self"* (Writers Club Press, 2000).

Disenhof, Carole S. *Talk the Weight Off!* (The All Cities Library, 2007).

Burns, David S., MD. *The Feeling Good Handbook* (The Penguin Group, 1999).

CDs

Bodhipaksa. *Guided Meditation for Calmness, Awareness and Love.*

Kabat-Zinn, Jon. *Guided Mindfulness Meditation – Series 1.*

Siegel, Bernie. *Meditation for Peace of Mind.*

Reilly, John L., PhD. *Progressive Deep Muscle Relaxation.*

Salredo, Beth, MD. *Progressive Muscle Relaxation.*

DVDs

Gaiam. *AM/PM Yoga.*

Gaiam. *Rodney Yee's Yoga for Beginners.*

Body Wisdom Media. *Yoga for Beginners.*

Websites

www.agpa.org – American Group Psychotherapy Association

www.apa.org – American Psychological Association

www.beckinstitute.org – Cognitive Behavioral Therapy information

www.BeyondHunger.org

www.eatright.org – Academy of Nutrition and Dietetics

www.GaiamTV.com – yoga online

www.GeneenRoth.com

www.PsychotherapyforWeightLoss.com

www.OvercomingOvereating.com

www.YogaFit.com – yoga DVDs and CDs

ABOUT THE AUTHOR

Dr. Sheila H. Forman is a clinical psychologist who specializes in helping people eliminate the emotional obstacles that prevent them from achieving their ideal weight. She is the author of two other self-help books, *Do You Use Food to Cope? A Comprehensive 15-Week Program for Overcoming Emotional Overeating* and *Self-Fullness: The Art of Loving and Caring for Your "Self."* Both books are available on amazon.com.

In addition, Dr. Sheila's other credentials include being a university professor, a radio talk show host, a media psychologist, and a lawyer.

For more information on Dr. Sheila, check out www. PsychotherapyforWeightLoss.com.

CPSIA information can be obtained
at www.ICGtesting.com
Printed in the USA
FSOW02n1839150415
6481FS